Popular Day Hikes 2

Canadian Rockies

Tony Daffern

Rocky
Mountain Books
VANCOUVER • VICTORIA • CALGARY

Rocky Mountain Books
#108 – 17665 66A Avenue
Surrey, BC V3S 2A7
www.rmbooks.com

Rocky Mountain Books
PO Box 468
Custer, WA
98240-0468

Library and Archives Canada Cataloguing in Publication

Daffern, Tony, 1938-
   Canadian Rockies / Tony Daffern.
(Popular day hikes ; 2)
ISBN 978-1-897522-01-1

   1. Hiking—Rocky Mountains, Canadian (B.C. and Alta.)—Guidebooks. 2. Trails—Rocky Mountains, Canadian (B.C. and Alta.)—Guidebooks. 3. Rocky Mountains, Canadian (B.C. and Alta.)—Guidebooks. I. Title. II. Series.

GV199.44.C22R627 2008 917.1104'5 C2007-907286-0

Library of Congress Control Number: 2007943171

Book design by Tony Daffern
Cover design by Chyla Cardinal
Proofread by Joe Wilderson
All cover and interior photos provided by Tony & Gillean Daffern unless otherwise noted.
Printed in China

Rocky Mountain Books acknowledges the financial support for its publishing program from the Government of Canada through the Book Publishing Industry Development Program (BPIDP), Canada Council for the Arts, and the province of British Columbia through the British Columbia Arts Council and the Book Publishing Tax Credit.

This book has been produced on 100% post-consumer recycled paper, processed chlorine free and printed with vegetable-based dyes.

Disclaimer

The actions described in this book may be considered inherently dangerous activities. Individuals undertake these activities at their own risk. The information put forth in this guide has been collected from a variety of sources and is not guaranteed to be completely accurate or reliable. Many conditions and some information may change owing to weather and numerous other factors beyond the control of the authors and publishers. Individual climbers and/or hikers must determine the risks, use their own judgment, and take full responsibility for their actions. Do not depend on any information found in this book for your own personal safety. Your safety depends on your own good judgment based on your skills, education, and experience.

   It is up to the users of this guidebook to acquire the necessary skills for safe experiences and to exercise caution in potentially hazardous areas. The authors and publishers of this guide accept no responsibility for your actions or the results that occur from another's actions, choices, or judgments. If you have any doubt as to your safety or your ability to attempt anything described in this guidebook, do not attempt it.

Introduction

Hiking in the Canadian Rockies

The Canadian Rockies is an area of high limestone peaks (up to 3954 m), glaciers, waterfalls, blue-green lakes, boisterous streams and forested valley bottoms of spruce and fir with larches at treeline.

Alpine meadows are the reward for hiking up through sometimes dense forest. For too brief a time, from early July to mid-August, they are crammed with flowers. In particular, overseas visitors will be intoxicated by the gaudy colours of North America's Indian Paintbrush. I advise all flower buffs to buy a field guide to put in the pack.

Getting to the trailhead

See the map on page 6. Other than a few buses that run along the Trans-Canada Highway and from Banff to Jasper, there is no public transportation, I have included one trail in both Banff and Jasper where you can walk or ride town transit to the trailhead. You can also walk up to the lake if you are staying in Lake Louise Village. For all other trails, you need a car.

Weather

The higher elevations trails of the Canadian Rockies enjoy a very short hiking season. Winter snowfall can be heavy, so many trails are not completely clear of snow until mid-July. Hiking usually starts in mid-May on lower elevation trails. In May there is usually a period of warm sunny weather. Rains fall mainly in June–the peak run-off time. During July and August temperatures can reach the mid 30s and there may be late afternoon thunderstorms. However, snow can fall in any month of the year and conditions at higher elevations can be really foul. The weather starts cooling off in mid-September. Indian summers can occur in late September through October and are glorious, bringing sunny stable weather. By the end of October, there is usually too much snow at higher elevations for hiking.

Drinking Water

Most locals drink from the creeks. However, there is a chance the water, especially at lower elevations, may be contaminated by *Giardia lamblia*, a parasite that can cause severe gastrointestinal distress. It is best to carry water from your home, hotel or campground.

Wildlife Concerns

It is unlikely that you will encounter bears if you are hiking these popular trails during normal daytime hiking hours. Having said that you should constantly be alert for signs of bears (tracks, scat), particularly in early fall when the berries ripen. Parks Canada will often close a trail until a bear has moved out of the area. See the Group Access information for the Moraine Lake Area on page 53, which requires hikers to travel in tight groups of four. Make a lot of noise if you suspect there is a bear in the area.

Elk and moose should also be given a wide berth, especially in fall during the mating season, when males get very ornery. Lately, cougars have become a year-round worry. However, they are rarely seen, as are wolves. Be wary of picas, ground squirrels and chipmunks. They bite and could carry disease.

Dogs in Jasper National Park

Dogs are not allowed on trails in Jasper National Park in important caribou habitat, in order to reduce stress on this threatened species. Dogs are not allowed on any of the trails in the Maligne Lake area nor at Cavell Meadows.

Lake O'Hara

Lake O'Hara is only accessible by pre-booking a bus or by hiking 11 km up the access trail. The bus service runs from mid-June to the end of September. The first bus leaves at 8:30 in the morning and the last bus out is at 6:30 in the evening—ample time for a good day's hiking. To book a spot on the bus call Parks Canada at 250-343-6433. Be sure to arrive early. Bus reservations become invalid 10 minutes before departure time and may be given away.

In order to fully appreciate this beautiful area you may choose to use one of the two accommodation options available to those who have not booked in at the Lodge a long time in advance.

Camping

Campground reservations may be made up to three months in advance by calling Parks Canada at 250-343-6433. Your campground reservation also secures you a place on the bus. Visit Parks Canada's web site www.pc.gc.ca/pn-np/bc/yoho/index_e.asp and follow links >activities>summer>Lake O'Hara for more information.

Elizabeth Parker Hut

You can stay at the Alpine Club of Canada's Elizabeth Parker Hut if space is available. Call 403-678-3200 for reservations. Your reservation also secures you a place on the bus. Be sure to visit www.alpineclubofcanada.ca before you consider this option. Follow links >Clubhouse and Alpine Huts>Overview.

Le Relais Day Shelter

Operated by the Lake O'Hara Trails Club, this small concession provides trail information, hot drinks and snacks (cash only).

Bus schedule

To O'Hara 8:30, 10:30 a.m. and 3:30, 5:30 p.m. From O'Hara 9:30, 11:30 a.m. and 2 :30, 4:30, 6:30 p.m.

Sunshine Meadows Alpine Shuttle

Access to the Sunshine Meadows is via a shuttle bus service run by White Mountain Adventures. No pets.

Shuttles leave from Sunshine Village parking lot. They depart every hour from 9:00 a.m. and return on the half-hour until 5:30 p.m. Fares in 2007, $24 adults, $14 children 3-12. Go anytime after 10:30 and children ride the shuttle for free! Reservations are not required.

There is one bus a day from Banff at 8:30 a.m. (reservation required) and two that return to Banff at 2:30 & 4:30 p.m. For more information call 403-762-7889 or view their web site at www.whitemountainadventures.com.

Safety tips

- It is safer to travel with company. If you travel alone, let someone know where you are going and when you expect to return. Research has shown that bears very rarely attack groups of four or more.
- Unless you are a seasoned hiker who knows the area well, going off trail can be fraught with dangers. Rock is usually friable and rockfall common.
- Start early, especially during the summer thunderstorm season. Carry a flashlight or headlamp when the days become shorter.
- Read the excellent Parks Canada pamphlet on what to do if you encounter a bear or cougar.
- Stay on the trail and resist the temptation to take perceived shortcuts.
- Carry a cellphone.

Regulations

There are very few regulations that apply to day hikers.
- Dogs must be kept on a leash.
- No dogs on some Jasper Area trails.
- Group Access (see page 53) may apply in the Moraine Lake area.

Using this book

How the trails were chosen

For their popularity, first of all. You are not likely to be alone. They are easily accessible from a road, start from parking lots that usually have biffies and picnic tables and are generally well-marked. To give variety they range from short to long and from easy walks to scrambles.

Trails

In this book, most of the trails are obvious and have signposts at junctions. Above treeline watch for cairns or paint splodges on rocks. A few of the lower-elevation trails near Banff or Jasper are shared with mountain bikers and equestrians.

Options

Type in blue indicates Going Farther, Alternatives and Optional Returns.

Hazard or regulations

Occasional red typo is used to convey a warning either of hazard or a regulation that must be followed.

Numbers in text

For clarity the text is written in short, numbered paragraphs. Numbers in the photo captions refer back to the paragraph numbers. Numbers in photo captions with an O in front of them refer to the option.

Difficulty

Describes conditions underfoot and the steepness of the grades. Scramble steps are noted. A few of the Going Farthers involve scrambling or going off trail.

Except after rain or during run-off, minor creek crossings can usually be jumped or crossed on rocks. All major creeks are bridged.

Distances

Distances are round trip, car to car, from the exit of the parking lot to the end of the trail as described in this guide.

Height gain

Height gains in this guide are total height gains for the round trip and include any significant height gained on the return.

Sketch maps

Red lines indicate main trails. Red-dashed lines are options. Black-dashed lines are other trails and are generally only shown where they intersect the red trails. Distances and positions of red lines were obtained using GPS track logs. Black-dashed lines are not guaranteed to be accurate. North is at the top of all maps. Contour interval is 100 m.

Do I need other maps?

Providing you stay on the trail it's possible to hike the trails using the maps in this book. Gem Trek publishes maps that cover all of the trails here, but you need to buy a lot of maps to cover them. Gem Trek maps are available at most outdoor stores, bookstores and gas stations in the region.

What to wear for the trails

Be prepared for fast weather changes and pack raingear. For walks and scrambles above treeline take a wind jacket, long pants and extra warm clothing. During the summer a sun hat, sun cream and mosquito repellent are must-takes. Light hiking boots suffice for all the trails in this book. Heavier boots are to be preferred on some of the scrambling options.

Doing more

If you have enjoyed the trails in this book and wish to hike in other areas of the Canadian Rockies consider Kananaskis Country, located south and west of Calgary in the eastern foothills of the Rockies, stretching from the Trans-Canada Highway to south of Longview.

A companion book to this one, *Popular Day Hikes 1: Kananaskis Country* by Gillean Daffern features 35 hikes throughout Kananaskis Country.

Area Map

Pocahontas

36
Miette
Hot Springs

16 37 32
F Jasper
31

35 33
34

Maligne
Lake

JASPER
NATIONAL
PARK

93

Columbia E 28
Icefield 26
27

Saskatchewan
River
Crossing

11

25

INFORMATION CENTRES

A Banff National Park
B Lake Louise
C Kootenay Park Lodge
D Yoho National Park
E Columbia Icefield
F Jasper National Park

24
23

YOHO
NATIONAL 16 17
PARK 15

21
22

D 9 11
Field 10 12
18 13 14
19 20

93

Lake
Louise

BANFF
NATIONAL
PARK

B

1A

6

Golden

1

Banff

KOOTENAY
NATIONAL
PARK

93

C

8

7

4 2 3

A 1

5

1

The Trails

Banff Area

Kootenay National Park

Lake Louise and Moraine Lake

Yoho National Park

Icefields Parkway

Jasper Area

1 Spray River Loop

Distance 11.5 km loop
Height gain 120 m
High point 1460 m
Moderate
Year-round

A pleasant walk with views of the Spray River and the long ridge of Mount Rundle. The only day hike in the Banff area that can be accessed by public transportation.

Start: Cross the bridge over the Bow River at the south end of Banff Avenue. Turn left. Keep left at the next traffic light and drive to the Banff Springs Hotel. Keep right around the traffic circle and pass under the bridge. Follow the road, bearing right past the staff parking, to its end at Spray River trailhead parking.

If you are in Banff without your own transportation you can ride the Banff Public Transit bus to the Banff Springs Hotel. Check with your hotel or the Information Centre for routes and schedules.

Difficulty: An easy trail following old fire roads that you will share with mountain bikers. In winter it is groomed and trackset with tracks on either side leaving space for you to walk in the middle. It can get very icy, so hiking poles are in order.

4. Turn left toward the river and descend a few feet to the bridge. Beyond the bridge, the trail climbs gently for the next three kilometres, passing Mount Rundle campsite after about half a kilometre.

5. Keep your eyes open for a trail sign on your left indicating the start of Old Quarry Loop.

6. Turn left and follow the trail as it traverses down across a steep bank toward the river. You can see the bridge downstream that you will be crossing shortly. A couple of switchbacks bring you down to river level where the trail follows the river edge to the bridge.

7. Cross the bridge and climb the bank to the trail junction mentioned in 1. Turn right to return to the trailhead.

1. Follow the wide trail on the west side of the Spray River through spruce and pine forest to a trail junction at 0.7 km. The trail to the left leads down to the river and will be your return route.

2. Keep straight ahead for now. Just after the top of the first climb look for a horse trail to the left. It makes a pleasant alternative to the fire road for the next kilometre. At a junction near the river, keep right and climb back up to the fire road.

3. The road finally descends, and the forest opens up to allow views of the river and the long ridge of Mount Rundle to your left. Arrive at a junction and picnic area. The trail straight ahead continues up the Spray River valley (see option).

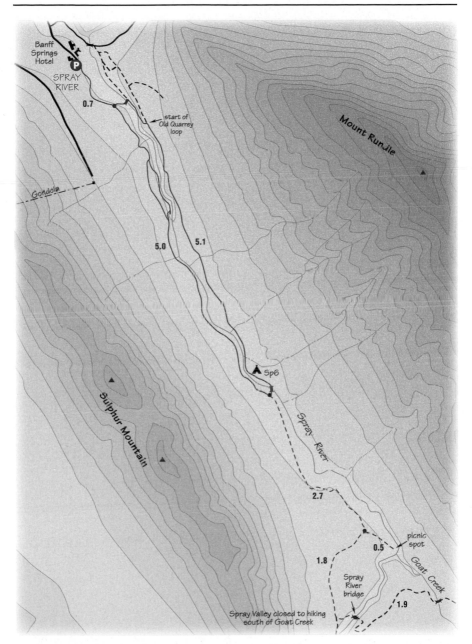

Banff
Springs
Hotel

SPRAY
RIVER

0.7

start of
Old Quarrey
loop

Gondole

Mount Runjle

5.0   5.1

Sulphur Mountain

Sp6

Spray River

2.7

picnic
spot

0.5

1.8

Goat Creek

Spray
River
bridge

1.9

Spray Valley closed to hiking
south of Goat Creek

*Opposite: View of the Banff Springs
Hotel from the top of the bank near
the start of Old Quarry Loop (6).*

The bridge over the Spray River (4).

Going farther up the Spray Valley

Add 6.4 km to picnic spot, 9 km to Spray River bridge and about 120 m height gain.

You can wander farther up the Spray Valley into Kananaskis Country. However, a logical turn-around point is the bridge over the Spray River. The Spray Valley beyond Goat Creek has been closed to travel in recent years as a result of the Park's bear management program.

1. At the end of 3, continue straight ahead, following the gradually ascending Spray Valley for 2.7 km to an obvious junction on the left.

2. Here you have the option of turning left and descending to a picnic spot by the river or carrying straight on to the bridge over the Spray River. If the latter, keep left at a junction where your trail leaves the main Spray Valley fire road.

3. Return the way you came, turning right across the river when you regain the main loop at (4).

Mount Rundle from the Spray River Bridge at O2.

2 Cascade Amphitheatre

Distance 15 km return
Height gain 640 m
High point 2195 m
Moderately strenuous
July to mid-September

A demanding trail to an impressive amphitheatre tucked into the west side of Cascade Mountain. Alpine wildflowers, pikas, hoary marmots and occasional mountain goats are the attractions here.

Start: Follow the Mount Norquay road from the Banff west interchange to Ski Norquay ski area. Park at the far end of the large parking lot.

Difficulty: Easily downhill to start with following a ski area access road then a good trail to Forty Mile Creek. After crossing the creek there is a steady uphill climb with steep zigzags for the last 2 km to the amphitheatre. On the return there is a 155 m climb back up to the ski area.

1. From the parking lot walk between the day lodge and service buildings and follow the gravel road past Cascade Chair for 1.2 km to Mystic Chair. Ignore a hiking sign just before Spirit Chair. The overgrown trail it indicates does not save height gain or distance.

2. The trail to Forty Mile Creek starts a few metres beyond the chairlift. After a short uphill, head steadily downhill to a junction. Trail to Mystic Lake to left. Keep right and continue downhill to Forty Mile Creek. Turn left across the bridge onto Elk Lakes trail.

3. Climb steadily for 1.5 km to another junction. The trail to Elk Lakes heads off left. Bear right for the Cascade Amphitheatre.

4. The trail climbs moderately, with occasional steep sections, in a series of large switchbacks through thick forest until it suddenly flattens out at the start of the amphitheatre.

Cascade Amphitheatre from the summit ridge of Cascade Mountain.

5. The trail continues through subalpine forest and flower meadows to the head of the amphitheatre just beyond the last trees and by a tiny creek. Trails to the right are climber's trails for the ascent of Cascade Mountain.

6. Return the way you came.

Top: A much foreshortened view of the summit of Cascade Mountain from near the last trees. The False Summit is seen in profile to the right.

This golden-mantled ground squirrel appeared within a few minutes of my sitting down by the tiny creek near the head of the cirque.

Option: Cascade Mountain

Height gain 820 m from amphitheatre
High point 2998 m

From the amphitheatre, the right-hand ridge appears an obvious and easy way to the summit. It is, however, a moderately difficult scramble and a much more serious undertaking than hiking the trail. It involves loose scree and talus and potentially tricky routefinding. It should only be attempted by experienced scramblers.

If you think you will be tempted to make the ascent once at the amphitheatre, you should request a copy of the excellent pamphlet *A Climber's Guide to Cascade Mountain* from the Information Centre in Banff.

The climb should only be attempted in good weather and after the winter snow has melted. Check the left skyline ridge as viewed from Banff Avenue for snow before you make a decision. It is usually clear of snow by early to mid July.

1. There are several trails accessing the ridge. The most straightforward is a narrow trail to the right as soon as the main trail levels out to enter the amphitheatre. Follow this uphill for about 150 m to a junction. Turn right. Straight on leads back to the main trail. Climb steeply onto the ridge.

2. Continue up the rocky ridge, which is treed to start with, and over the first bump on an easy dirt trail and over rocks. Don't follow a tempting cairned route to the right. Stick to the ridge, scrambling down the far side of the first bump. From here, start to look behind you frequently so as to memorize the route for your descent.

3. Continue up zigzags on grass and rock until you reach a section of moderately steep rock slabs at the edge of a cliffband. Scramble down a couple of metres to the right and continue just below the ridgeline. This descent is the key to accessing the traverse line to the right across the slopes of the False Summit. Note the descent location for your return.

4. Continue upward, watching for another short downclimb that allows you to access the start of the False Summit traverse. Follow the good (except for a couple of smooth, gritty slabs) trail that leads right for 150 m to the right-hand skyline. Note where the trail reaches the ridge for your descent.

5. Scramble down a couple of metres and climb loose scree up along the base of the cliff to a ridge at the edge of a steep bowl. Cross the steep, exposed bowl on a good, though narrow trail to the main ridge beyond the False Summit. This section is potentially very dangerous when snow covered—consider turning back.

6. Follow the ridge up steep, loose talus to the top.

7. Descend exactly the same way as you came up. Do not attempt **any** shortcuts however tempting. Take your time—it is easy to get off route, with potentially serious consequences. There are three places that require particular routefinding attention.

8. Make sure that you locate the top of the False Summit traverse line (4). It is at the highest point at which it is possible to cross the ridge, and the traverse is immediately visible when you scramble onto the ridge. Do not follow a false trail that leads to a small saddle lower down.

9. Take time to locate the route up the cliffband to the foot of the slabs mentioned in (3).

10. After descending the ridge from the slabs, scramble up to the top of the first bump and descend the ridge. There is an inviting traverse trail to the left, but this route necessitates a long rightward traverse across loose boulders to regain the ascent ridge. See the black-dashed line on map.

11. Continue down the ridge to the main amphitheatre trail.

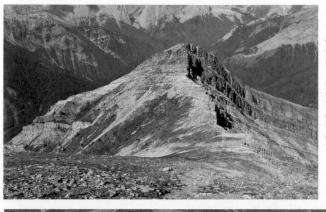

The summit side of the first bump. It is best to traverse directly over the bump on both ascent and descent. The well-used trail to the left requires a long traverse back to the ridge above the amphitheatre, which swings to the right. The trail to the left could lead you significantly off route when visibility is bad.

This photo shows the route described in O3&4. It is the key to a trouble-free ascent.

The traverse around the False Summit (O4).

The back side of the False Summit. There is a big drop-off at bottom left so be prepared to back off if the slope is snow covered.

A foreshortened view of the summit ridge from the back of the False Summit.

This mountain goat appeared around the rock on the right in the photo below just a few seconds after I had taken the picture—startling us both.

Lake Minnewanka from the summit. The prominent peaks across the lake are Mount Inglismaldie (left) and Mount Girouard.

15

3 C-Level Cirque

Distance 9.4 km return
Height gain 455 m
High point 1920 m
Moderately strenuous
Mid-June to end of September

Start: Follow the Lake Minnewanka road from the Banff east interchange for 3.5 km and turn left into the Upper Bankhead picnic site. The trail starts at the far west (left as you drive in) corner of the parking lot.

Difficulty: A good, moderately steep trail all the way.

A classic scree and boulder-strewn Canadian Rockies cirque carved into the cliffs of Cascade Mountain.

1. The trail follows an old mine access track through the forest to the old C-Level shaft, passing the remains of an old mine building on the way.

2. From the building a trail to the right climbs up onto the tailings pile to a viewpoint offering good views of Lake Minnewanka backdropped by the Fairholme Range and the Bow Valley with Mount Rundle in the background.

3. The trail continues climbing past old fenced-off mine workings (take either trail at a fork), then enters dense forest that persists until shortly before you reach the rocky knoll at the entrance to the cirque.

4. Descend slightly to the right and follow a narrow, moderately steep trail to a rocky bench. Large boulders provide good seating while you admire the view.

5. Return the way you came.

Note: It is possible, but not recommended, to scramble through trees and up scree at the right-hand edge of the cirque until high enough for good views of Lake Minnewanka and the Bow Valley.

Old mine building a short way up the trail. A trail to the right leads to a tailing pile with good views.

The upper slopes of the cirque are still snowbound in mid-June.

17

Starting the descent from the rocky bench (4).

Looking down from the upper trail toward the rocky knoll (3).

Lake Minnewanka from the right-hand edge of the cirque. Mount Inglismaldie reaching into the cloud at centre right.

4 Cory Pass–Edith Pass Circuit

Distance 13.7 km loop
Height gain 1035 m
High point 2350 m
Very strenuous
Mid-July to mid-September

The premier hike in the Banff area takes you across a high pass, under the nearly vertical southeast face of Mount Louis and around the rocky pinnacles of Mount Edith.

Start: Drive west from Banff on the Trans-Canada Highway. Turn right onto the 1A Parkway 5.7 km west of the Norquay interchange. After 300 m turn right and follow the road to its end at the Fireside Picnic Area.

Difficulty: An arduous, leg-numbing 925 m ascent to Cory Pass in one direction; a toe-jamming descent if you hike the circuit in the other direction. Some prefer to get the hard part over early in the day. Photographers prefer the anticlockwise direction to get the best light on the mountains. Whichever direction you choose, it is an outing for tough, experienced hikers.

Clockwise

1. From the trailhead cross the creek, turn right, and follow an old road 300 m downhill. Turn left onto a good trail and proceed to the Cory Pass/Edith Pass trail junction. To hike the circuit clockwise (Cory Pass first) turn left; otherwise go straight on.

2. The trail begins a long, steep uphill climb on an open south-facing slope—a good reason to start early—then switchbacks through trees onto the end of Mount Edith's south ridge.

3. Continue easily along the ridge through trees with views ahead of Mount Edith and Cory Pass. A short uphill precedes a downhill scramble to a small col between the ridge and Mount Edith. The rock is polished and care must be taken.

4. From the base of the rock step follow the trail up the ridge through trees a short way before embarking on a long, rising traverse to Cory pass across generally open slopes.

The trail is sometimes sketchy where it crosses shale gullies. Ignore a climber's trail to the right. Arrive at the pass, a rocky defile with a good view of Mount Edith.

5. After a well-deserved rest, descend the steep talus slope on the north side of the pass. A little way down you get the first view of the impressive southeast face of Mount Louis. After the initial steep descent the grade eases off on a long, descending traverse to the right on scree slopes above Gargoyle Valley. Arrive at a jumble of boulders at the narrowest part of the valley between the sheer faces of mounts Edith and Louis.

6. From here pick your way down the rocky defile, following cairns traversing rightward on scree to the start of the 60 m climb around Edith's north ridge. Climb across a scree slope, taking a right-hand option low down. Continue into trees—sign—and climb through forest to a high point. Note a climber's trail to the right. Carry straight on, making a descending traverse across avalanche slopes on the northeast slope of Mount Edith. A steeper descent through ever-increasing trees brings you to the environs of forested Edith Pass.

7. Continue down through trees to the main Edith Pass trail. To the left is the trail to Forty Mile Creek. Turn right.

8. Continue down the shady valley through mossy forest following the line of the stream for 3 km to a point close to the highway. Here the trail turns right, crosses Edith Creek and ascends a short hill to the Cory Pass/Edith Pass trail junction and the completion of the circuit. Carry straight on to the trailhead in 1.2 km.

Top left: The partially forested slopes below Mount Edith leading to Cory Pass.

Top right: The sometimes sketchy trail in the last kilometre before the pass.

Right: The short downhill scramble mentioned in 3.

The southeast face of Mount Louis from just below Cory Pass. Climbers descend to the col on the left, then pick their way down steep slopes to Gargoyle Valley.
Photo: Gillian Ford.

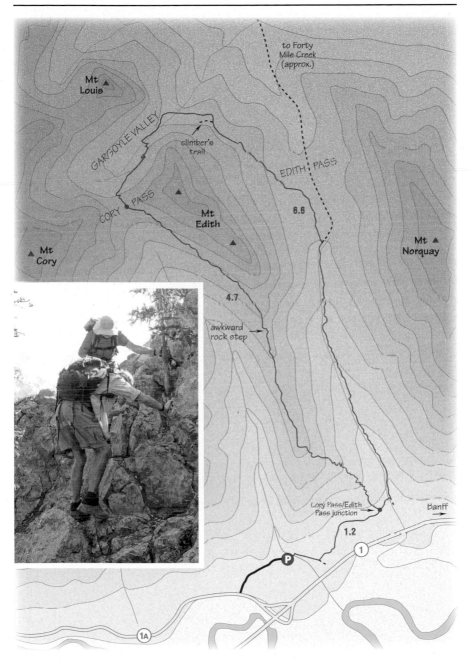

Mt Louis

to Forty Mile Creek (approx.)

GARGOYLE VALLEY

climber's trail

EDITH PASS

CORY PASS

Mt Edith

6.6

Mt Norquay

Mt Cory

4.7

awkward rock step

Cory Pass/Edith Pass junction

Banff

1.2

1

P

1A

21

Above: The trail stays high above the right-hand side of Gargoyle Valley until it descends to a jumble of boulders below the north buttress of Mount Edith.

Mount Louis from the scree slope at the start of the climb around Mount Edith's north ridge (6).

5 Sunshine Meadows

Distance 11.3 km loop
Height gain 160 m
High point 2305 m
Moderate
Shuttle bus June 15 to Sept. 30

Flower-filled subalpine meadows with unobstructed views, deep blue lakes, picturesque islets and a distant view of Mount Assiniboine.

Start: From Banff head west on the Trans-Canada Hwy. 8 km and turn off at the Sunshine Village exit. Follow the road 7 km to the far end of the large parking lot. The shuttle bus ticket office is on the lower floor of the building on the left and opens at 8:30 a.m. daily.

Sunshine Meadows Alpine Shuttle
See page 4 for shuttle information.

At the village there is a small deli where you can purchase drinks and snacks.

Difficulty: Good, well-maintained trails suitable for all ages.

1. Follow a wide gravel track uphill from the centre of the village. Turn left just past the Avalanche Control log cabin (signed).

2. The trail climbs steadily uphill through the ski area meadows to the Great Divide—the boundary between Alberta and British Columbia. Ignore a trail to the left that goes to the base of a chairlift. Arrive at a junction. The trail to the left goes to Citadel Pass about 8 km away. Keep right to Rock Isle Lake.

3. You soon reach the Rock Isle Lake viewpoint. Carry on around the lake, noting two trails to the right to Twin Cairns. Keep left and descend to Rock Isle Lake's outlet stream. From here you can see Grizzly and Larix lakes below. Descend to a junction marking the start of a loop around the two lakes. You can go either way. Don't miss the Simpson Viewpoint.

4. Having completed the loop, head back up to Rock Isle Lake to the previously noted Twin Cairns junction. If you turn right you will return directly to Sunshine Village, but miss out on a great viewpoint. Turn left.

5. The trail heads toward the valley between Twin Cairns and Standish Ridge. At the next junction turn right and climb fairly steeply to Standish Viewpoint, where you are treated to expansive views of the Sunshine meadows.

6. Return to the junction with Twin Cairns trail and turn right. Follow the trail through flower meadows to the junction with the Simpson Pass trail. Monarch Viewpoint, with a view of Mount Ball, is about 200 m to the left. Turn right and return to Sunshine Village.

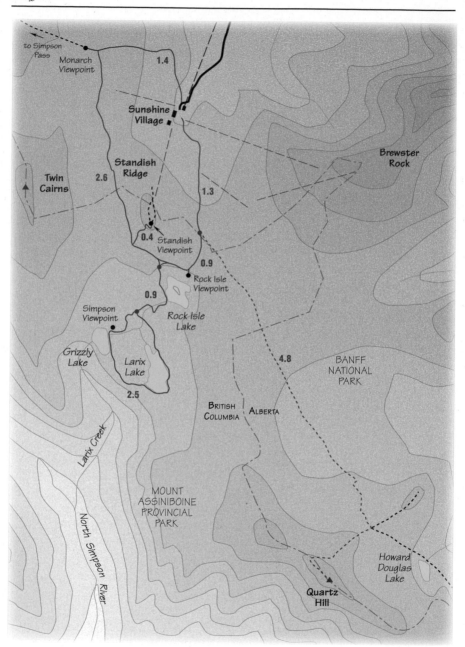

Rock Isle Lake. The sharply pointed peak in the centre distance is part of Split Peak in Kootenay National Park.

Rock Isle and Larix lakes from Standish Viewpoint. Mount Assiniboine is just visible between the summits of Quartz Hill.

Larix Lake back-dropped by the imposing wall of The Monarch.

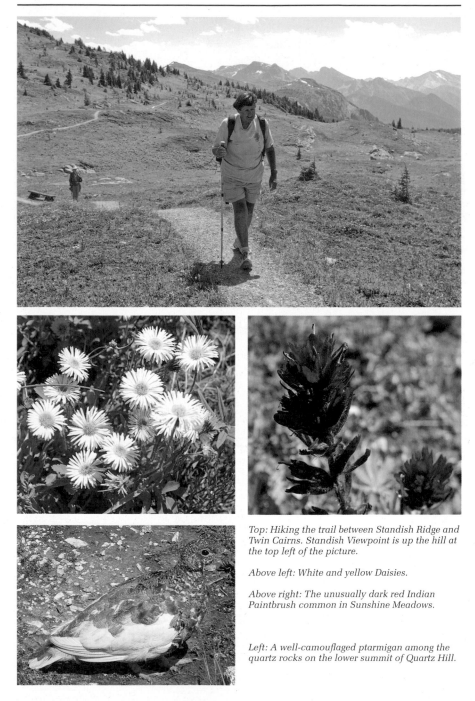

Top: Hiking the trail between Standish Ridge and Twin Cairns. Standish Viewpoint is up the hill at the top left of the picture.

Above left: White and yellow Daisies.

Above right: The unusually dark red Indian Paintbrush common in Sunshine Meadows.

Left: A well-camouflaged ptarmigan among the quartz rocks on the lower summit of Quartz Hill.

Option: Quartz Hill

Distance 12.2 km return from Sunshine
Height gain 195 m

If you want more of a wilderness experience than the often crowded hike to Rock Isle, Grizzly and Larix lakes, you can follow the Citadel Pass trail to the broad northeast ridge of Quartz Hill, then scramble to the top.

1. Turn left at the Rock Isle Lake-Citadel Pass junction (2) onto the Citadel Pass trail. The wider trail to the right goes to the lakes.

2. Head southeast across open, flower filled meadows. Descend slightly into a basin with occasional stands of larches, then climb steeply through heavier tree cover to the broad ridge. If you don't feel like scrambling to the top of Quartz Hill you can turn left here and enjoy the views from the end of the ridge.

3. From the ridge crest turn right and head straight up the ridge, keeping to the rocky areas as much as possible, to the foot of Quartz Hill. Climb directly up to the first group of rocks, then make a moderately steep, rising traverse to the right on grass

then scree, to the rocky northwest ridge. Scramble up the ridge to the twin summits and a magnificent 360° view.

4. Return the way you came.

Heading along the northeast ridge toward the higher summit of Quartz Hill (O3).

The higher peak of Quartz Hill has two small summits. Mount Assiniboine in the background.

27

6 Johnston Canyon to Inkpots

Distance 12.2 km return
Height gain 445 m
High point 1760 m
Moderate
June to October—middle to end of
June best for waterfalls.

A spectacular canyon with multiple waterfalls, tufa deposits, Black Swifts and Dippers. Continue to five quicksand-bottomed mineral ponds fed by karst springs.

Start: Drive west from Banff on the Trans-Canada Highway. Turn right onto the 1A Parkway 5.5 km west of the Norquay interchange. After 17.8 km turn right into a parking lot signed "Johnston Canyon" about 200 m before the Johnston Canyon Resort. From Lake Louise, drive toward Banff on either Hwy. 1 or 1A. The resort is 6.5 km east of Castle Junction. The trail starts at the far west corner of the parking lot.

Difficulty: A broad, paved trail with catwalks and viewpoints through the canyon followed by a good trail to the Inkpots.

1. A short trail crosses Johnston Creek to the resort. Turn right and follow the paved trail through the canyon enjoying the splendour and power of rushing water and roaring cascades. If you have not been here before it's worth it in spite of the crowds.

2. Continue beyond the upper falls, leaving the crowds behind, to a junction. Turn right onto an old fire road.

3. Continue climbing to the high point of the trail, then descend 115 m to meadows and the Inkpots to the right.

4. Return the way you came. If you wish to avoid the crowds in the canyon, keep right where you previously joined the fire road (2). Watch for a signed hiking trail to Moose Meadows to the right. Keep straight on down the fire road, ignoring any side trails. Follow the track along the back of the resort and round into the resort parking lot. Cross the bridge to your stating point.

Boardwalks provide the only access to the deep, narrow early sections of the canyon.

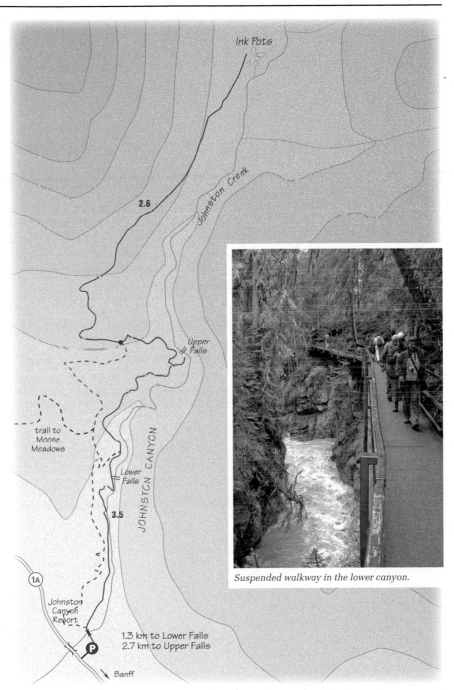

Ink Pots

Johnston Creek

2.6

Upper
Falls

trail to
Moose
Meadows

JOHNSTON CANYON

Lower
Falls

3.5

1A

Johnston
Canyon
Resort

P

1.3 km to Lower Falls
2.7 km to Upper Falls

Banff

Suspended walkway in the lower canyon.

Top left: The upper falls under normal runoff conditions.

Top right: The lower falls during a period of high runoff. Cross the bridge to view the falls through the tunnel on the other side. Photographers: note that direct sunlight only reaches into the canyon for a couple of hours around midday—when it is most crowded.

Spray from windblown water droplets and focused rays of sunshine in the narrow canyon combine to create frequent rainbow such as this one across the top of the upper falls.

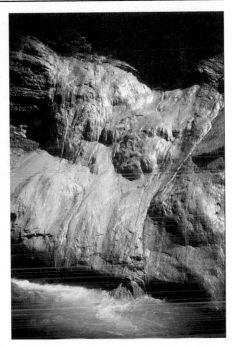

Spring water bubbles up through the gravel and sand to form the five pools. The colour of the pools depends on the amount of fine silty material on the bottom. The water remains at a constant temperature of about 4 °C throughout the year.

A colourful wall of tufa on the far side of the canyon

Enjoying a sunny day at the Inkpots. The mountain in the background is unnamed.

31

7 *Arnica Lake*

Distance 10 km return
Height gain 710 m
High point 2150 m
Strenuous
June to end of September

Start: From Castle Junction on the Trans-Canada Hwy., follow Hwy. 93 south toward Radium to the unsigned Vista Lake Viewpoint, 8.2 km west of Castle Junction. The viewpoint parking is 1.2 km west of Boom Lake trailhead. Be careful—there is no left-turn lane off the highway.

Difficulty: A good moderately steep trail that climbs relentlessly. There is a 120 m height gain from Vista Lake up to your vehicle at the end of the day.

1. Head down the narrow trail to Vista Lake and cross the bridge over the lake's outlet.

2. The trail now climbs relentlessly up the slopes of Storm Mountain through recent growth of lodgepole pine seeded after the 1968 fire. An open, lightly treed ridge

A tranquil blue-green lake set below steep cliffs.

gives good views to Castle Mountain and Mount Whymper. Pass into mature forest and arrive at a small tarn.

3. Sorry. This is not Arnica Lake. You still have 800 m and 80 m height gain to go. A short descent and you are at the lake.

3. Return the way you came.

Heartleaf Arnica, from which the lake gets its name.

Arnica Lake below the cliffs of Storm Mountain's northeast ridge.

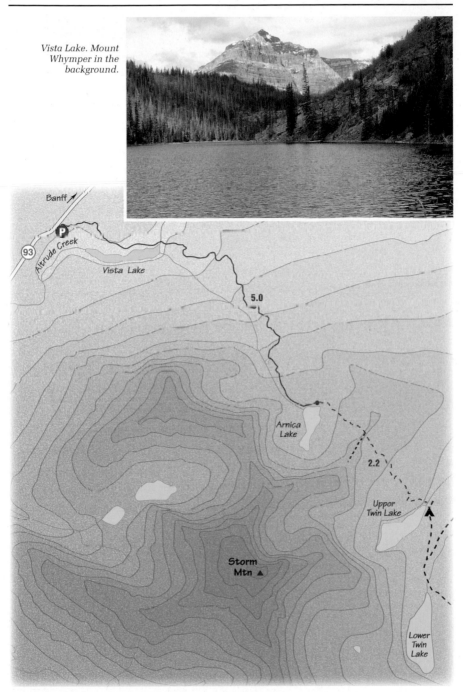

Vista Lake. Mount Whymper in the background.

Banff

93

Altrude Creek

Vista Lake

5.0

Arnica Lake

2.2

Uppor Twin Lake

Storm Mtn ▲

Lower Twin Lake

Going farther to Upper Twin Lake

Distance add 4.4 km
Height gain add 360 m

Extend your hike over a ridge to a larger, more colourful lake.

1. From Arnica Lake continue along the trail ascending 135 m to an attractive pass over a narrow, larch-forested ridge.

2. The trail now descends, steeply at first, to Upper Twin Lake, the more attractive of the two Twin Lakes. Cross the outlet creek on stepping stones to the campground.

3. Return the way you came.

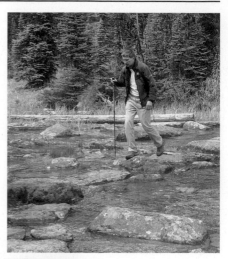

Above: Crossing the stepping stones shortly before the backcountry campground at Upper Twin Lake.

The pass between Arnica Lake and Upper Twin Lake in early summer. If you don't feel like going down to Twin Lake—and back up again—you can climb up the ridge to the right (southwest) until you get a good view across the Bow Valley to Castle Mountain.

Upper Twin Lake from near the campground. Storm Mountain is up to the right.

8 Stanley Glacier

Distance 9 km return
Height gain 335 m
High point 1920 m
Moderately strenuous
June to end of September

From fire to ice. Brilliant flowers bloom against a background of burned-black trees. A hanging valley with high peaks, a receding glacier and marmots.

Start: From Castle Junction on the Trans-Canada Hwy., follow Hwy. 93 south toward Radium to Stanley Glacier parking area 3.5 km west of the Alberta–British Columbia boundary.

Difficulty: Good, well-maintained trail, easy to moderate grades. Loose, rocky trail over talus moraines beyond the end of the official trail.

1. After crossing the bridge over the Vermilion River, the trail switchbacks steadily up through the burn area into the side valley containing Stanley Glacier. Cross a bridge over Stanley Creek.

This area was devastated by fire in the 1968 Vermilion Pass burn. By the turn of the century the new forest had attained a height of about 8–10 metres. In 2003,

in order to contain a massive fire to the west, this area was intentionally fired by Parks Canada. Note the blackened trees, still standing in 2007, and the larger charred deadfall from the earlier fire.

2. The grade soon eases as you follow the northeast side of the creek up the valley, crossing the occasional avalanche slope. This area was not touched by the 2003 fire; the young trees are regenerated growth after the fire in 1968.

3. The trees become more sparse as the trail enters an area of glacial moraine. The official trail ends on the crest of a moraine overlooking the rocky valley.

4. Return the way you came.

Approaching the end of the official trail. The triangular cliff band below the hanging valley is clearly visible in the centre of the picture.

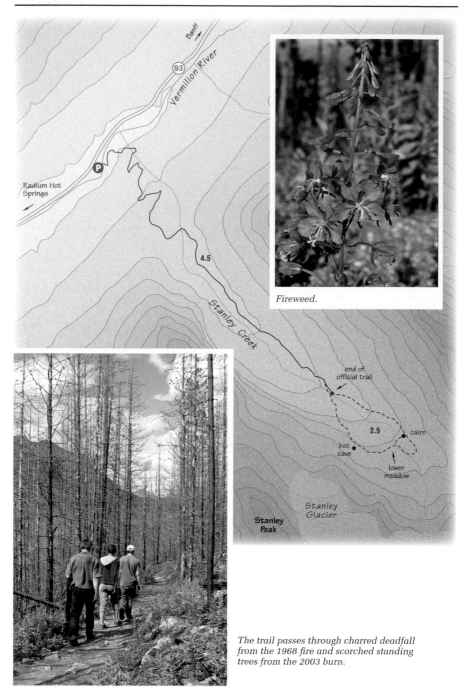

Fireweed.

The trail passes through charred deadfall from the 1968 fire and scorched standing trees from the 2003 burn.

Continue to a hanging valley

Distance add 2 km
Height gain add 200 m

From the end of the official trail you can see trails on either side leading to a hanging valley above a triangular cliff band. The trail to the left is the easiest way up, leaving the steeper one to the right for the descent.

1. Continue up the rocky trail trending left onto the left-hand of the two trails heading for a treed slope. The one you want is immediately below the moraine on the left. Follow this moderately steep trail through the trees and across scree up to the left of the cliffs below the hanging valley. Arrive at a cairn at cliff-top level.

2. From the cairn you can cross the ridge to your right and descend to the lower meadow, or you can continue on the same line and make a circuit of the treed ridge, descending by the creek to the lower meadow. From here you have great views of the Stanley Glacier and back down the valley.

3. Either descend the way you came (easier) or head toward the west side of the valley on a good trail and descend below the cliffs (some exposure across a rock band), below the bat cave and down to the end of the official trail.

Looking down on three different trails heading up toward the hanging valley from the end of the official trail. The upper trail, once you get on it, takes the best line up and across the slope.

The bat cave is worth taking a look at. In winter, mixed rock and ice climbers hang bat-like from ice climbing tools protected by the may bolts leading out from the roof of the cave.

9 Lake Agness–Beehives Circuit

Distance 13.7 km return
(Teahouse by shortest route 8.2 km)
Height gain 670 m
High point 2255 m
Moderately strenuous
Year round to Lake Agnes, summer
and fall to Big Beehive

Impressive viewpoints, sheer cliffs, a blue-green lake in an enclosed cirque and a teahouse. Chipmunks, pikas, marmots and ground squirrels.

Start: From Lake Louise Village follow the well-signed road uphill to Lake Louise and park in the large public parking lot. Head toward the Chateau, cross the bridge over the outlet creek and follow the lakeside path in front of the Chateau to the far end.

Difficulty: Good, well maintained trails that can be icy in winter. The switchbacks to Big Beehive provide a moderately angled route up a steep slope.

1. Fork right at a well-signed junction on the trail to Mirror Lake and Lake Agnes. Switchback up the broad, well-maintained trail, ignoring any junctions, to Mirror Lake. Turn right just before the lake.

2. Climb a few switchbacks to a junction where the trail to Little Beehive angles back to the right. Turn right.

3. After about 500 m note the trail heading back to the left. You will follow this trail to Lake Agnes on your return from Little Beehive. Pass the trail to Mount St. Piran on your left and climb to the crest of a ridge with views of both Lake Louise and Lake Agnes. Continue to Little Beehive viewpoint.

4. Retrace your steps past the Mount St. Piran junction to the aforementioned Lake Agnes connector trail, which reaches the lake just beyond the teahouse (open daily June to October from 10 a.m. to 6 p.m.). They serve soup, sandwiches, cookies and pastries as well as many varieties of black and herbal teas.

5. After a stop for refreshment follow the trail to the end of the lake. Note the

Lake Agnes Teahouse on a busy day at the end of June.

switchbacks up the slope to the left as you go. They can be quite difficult to ascend if there is a lot of snow on them. This is the route to Big Beehive.

6. Boulder-hop across the creek at the end of the lake and embark on the switchbacks. Using a slow and steady "guides" pace you will soon reach the saddle between Lake Agnes and Lake Louise. Head left on a rocky trail for about 400 m to the gazebo at the Big Beehive viewpoint.

7. Retrace your steps to the saddle and turn left. The trail descends steeply in a few lazy zigzags to the highline trail that runs between Mirror Lake and the Plain of the Six Glaciers. Turn left and follow the trail through forest to Mirror Lake.

8. Return the way you came.

Big Beehive from Mirror Lake.

Looking down on the Chateau Lake Louise from just below Little Beehive viewpoint. The view from here is better than at Little Beehive viewpoint.

Lake Agness on a dull day from near the Teahouse. Although it is the end of June, there is still a lot of snow around. The lower peak is Devil's Thumb, with higher Mount Whyte on the right.

The switchback trail leading to Big Beehive still has some snow on it (6). It can be tricky earlier in the season when completely snow covered.

Option: A two-teahouse day

If you are feeling energetic you can visit two teahouses in one day by turning right on the highline trail (7) and following its scenic route with views of mounts Victoria and Lefroy as it gently traverses to the Plain of the Six Glaciers trail. Stay high at the next intersection for the best views. Return via the Lake Louise Lakeshore Trail. See hike #10, Plain of the Six Glaciers.

Centre: The gazebo on the summit of Big Beehive is a good place to stop for a snack.

The Highline trail descends gently to the Plain of the Six Glaciers Trail with outstanding views of The Mitre (off to the left), Mount Lefroy and Mount Victoria.

10 *Plain of the Six Glaciers*

Distance 14.8 km return
Height gain 335 m
High point 2070 m
Moderately strenuous
Mid-June to end of September
Year-round to end of lake.

Start: From Lake Louise Village follow the well-signed road uphill to Lake Louise and park in the large public parking lot. Head toward the Chateau, cross the bridge over the outlet creek and follow the lakeside path in front of the Chateau to the far end.

Difficulty: Good, well-maintained trail, almost flat along the lake then steady climbing to teahouse. Well-trodden rocky moraine ending at a scree slope if you go farther.

1. Fork left at a well-signed junction and head around the lake on the scenic Lakeshore Trail. Shortly after you pass the cliffs at the end of the lake the trail begins to climb steadily through open forest and across avalanche slopes passing one junction with a shortcut trail leading to the

A stark landscape of moraine, snow, ice and glacier-clad Mount Victoria.

Highline Trail to Mirror Lake and another with the terminus of the Highline Trail. See the option on page 43.

2. The trail emerges into the alpine world of rocky moraines. A little steeper now, it heads across ledges and open hillsides. Just as you get on the moraine, the trail divides. The upper trail traverses rock ledges with a cable handrail. If you don't have a head for heights follow the lower trail. Make a few moderately steep switchbacks, then round a corner into a small patch of forest containing the teahouse (open daily July to September from 10 a.m. to 4 p.m.). Here you can get soup, sandwiches, apple pie and a variety of teas.

3. The trail continues up the crest of a lateral moraine gaining another 120 m of elevation from the teahouse to a viewpoint overlooking the Victoria Glacier and the "Death Trap" couloir between mounts Lefroy and Victoria.

4. Return the way you came.

The gentle trail along the lake. The quartzite cliff ahead is a popular rock climbing crag.

The upper and lower trails (?) If you don't have a head for heights, follow the lower trail.

Plain of the Six Glaciers Teahouse.

A more scenic option

Add 1.5 km and a little extra height gain.

Rather than hiking along the lakeshore each way, climb to Mirror Lake and follow the scenic Highline Trail to the Plain of the Six Glaciers.

1. Fork right at the end of the Chateau on the trail to Lake Agnes. At Mirror Lake head left on the Highline Trail. Keep straight on at all junctions, joining the Lakeshore Trail just before it reaches the moraine.

2. On your return, follow the Lakeshore Trail back to the Chateau.

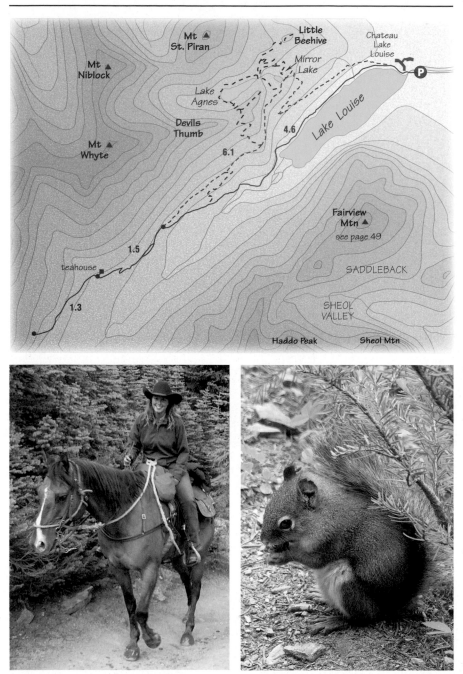

Mt
St. Piran

Little
Beehive

Chateau
Lake
Louise

Mt
Niblock

Mirror
Lake

Lake
Agnes

Lake Louise

Devils
Thumb

4.6

Mt
Whyte

6.1

Fairview
Mtn

see page 49

1.5

SADDLEBACK

teahouse

SHEOL
VALLEY

1.3

Haddo Peak

Sheol Mtn

You will share this trail with equestrians.

This Red Squirrel is used to hikers.

The final moraine ridge before the trail ends at the scree-slope viewpoint in the picture below (3). Lake Louise with Fairview Mountain (hike #12, page 49) to its right, is visible in the distance.

Looking into the "Death Trap" between Mount Lefroy on the left and Mount Victoria. Because of the danger from falling seracs, the Abbot Pass climbers hut on the col is usually accessed from the Lake O'Hara side.

11 Mount St. Piran

Distance 13.4 km
Height gain 915 m
High point 2649 m
Strenuous
Mid-June to end of September

Outstanding close-up views of rugged peaks and glaciers from one of the best hiker-accessible peaks in the area.

Start: From Lake Louise Village follow the well-signed road uphill to Lake Louise and park in the large public parking lot. Head toward the Chateau, cross the bridge over the outlet creek and follow the lakeside path in front of the Chateau to the far end.

Difficulty: Easy, well-maintained trail to start with, followed by moderately steep switchbacks and a final rocky scramble to the summit.

1. Fork right at a well-signed junction on the trail to Mirror Lake and Lake Agnes. The main trail heads around the lakeshore. Switchback up the broad, well-maintained path ignoring any junctions to Mirror Lake. Turn right just before the lake.

2. Climb a few switchbacks to a junction where the trail to Little Beehive angles back to the right. Head toward Little Beehive, passing a trail that heads back left toward Lake Agnes. Watch for the St. Piran trail to the left in another 250 m.

3. Head up through delicate larch forest with ever-increasing views, then follow moderately steep switchbacks to the summit ridge. From here, scramble over loose, slabby rock to the broad, multi-cairned summit.

4. Either descend the way you came, with a detour to the teahouse, or traverse the mountain to the St. Piran/Niblock col and descend to the teahouse. See the option on page 48.

Looking south toward Fairview Mountain on the left and mounts Haddo and Aberdeen, split by a glacier, on the right. The summit of Mount Temple is just visible in the background.

The summit of Mount St. Piran. The Daly Glacier backdropped by Mount Daly in the distance.

Mount Whyte (left) and Mount Niblock from the multi-cairned summit of Mount St. Piran.

Optional descent via St. Piran/ Niblock Col

You can traverse Mount St. Piran via the St. Piran/Niblock col, then descend to Lake Agnes. This route is more demanding as it involves descending a steep boulderfield then loose scree and dirt. It should not be attempted if the slope above the west end of Lake Agnes is snow covered.

1. Head southwest toward Mount Niblock and descend loose rock to the St. Piran/ Niblock Col.

2. Head down the steep, convex slope toward Lake Agnes. The trail initially trends right, then heads straight down to the rocky valley below, which is followed to the lake and teahouse.

Mount Niblock with the St. Piran/Niblock col out of sight to the right. On the descent from the col you need to trend right toward the head of the valley before descending to avoid the obvious cliffbands.

12 Fairview Mountain

Distance 10.4 km
Height gain 1014 m
High point 2745 m
Strenuous
July to end of September

Delicate larches. Marmots and pikas and an incredible panorama of high glaciated peaks.

Start: From Lake Louise Village follow the well-signed road uphill to Lake Louise and park in the large public parking lot. Head toward the Chateau and look for a signed trail that heads into the forest near the viewpoint seats. If you park in the upper-level lot there is a trail from the west corner that joins the Fairview trail a short distance up from the trailhead (turn left).

Difficulty: A good, though moderately steep, trail to Saddleback. The ascent of Fairview Mountain is steep rock and scree with snow patches early in the season.

Looking back toward Lake Louise from the open slopes of the Saddleback.

1. Initially, the trail passes a number of junctions, including one to the upper parking lot after about 100 m and one to the right to Fairview Lookout. Keep straight. Another junction a short distance beyond the Lookout junction leads to Paradise Valley and Moraine Lake. Bear right.

2. The trail now begins a sustained but moderate climb through forest and across avalanche slopes toward the Saddleback. At one point the trail briefly divides; stay left. The trail emerges into meadows and open larch forest and makes some final zigzags to the pass.

3. From the pass follow a trail to the right up an open slope toward the highest stands of larches. From here an obvious trail, with many variations, zigzags steeply up rock and scree to the summit.

4. Descend the way you came. It is quicker and easier than any of the steeper "short-cut" routes back to the Saddleback.

Note: Do not, under any circumstances, attempt to descend directly to Lake Louise. The north ridge of Fairview Mountain is loose and very steep, with hidden cliffbands. It has been the scene of fatalities and many rescues.

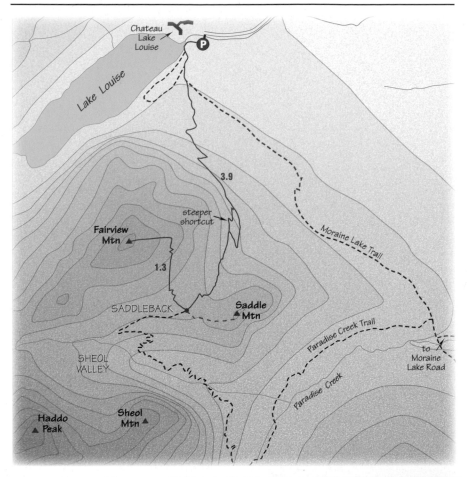

Note: It is possible to return to Lake Louise from Saddleback via Sheol Valley, Paradise Valley and Moraine Lake Trail. However, Sheol and Paradise valleys are subject to Group Access Regulations. Read "Group Access" on page 53 before considering this option.

Looking down onto Saddleback and Saddle Mountain from the route up Fairview Mountain. Sheol Valley beyond.

The route up Fairview from Saddle Mountain can be seen as a rising traverse from left to right. It is best to descend by your ascent route rather than by the steeper route to the right.

Mount Victoria from the summit of Fairview Mountain.

51

Saddle Mountain from the Saddleback.

Easier option to Saddle Mountain

Distance 0.7 km from Saddleback
Height gain 90 m above Saddleback

This little peak is often passed over in favour of the higher Fairview Mountain. It offers superb views down to Lake Annette and across to the massive bulk of Mount Temple. An option for hikers who don't want the steep, loose scramble up Fairview Mountain.

1. Scramble to the twin summits from the height of land.

2. Descend the way you came. Make sure you stay on the easy-angled ridge when you leave the summit by avoiding false trails that lead onto steep ground to the left.

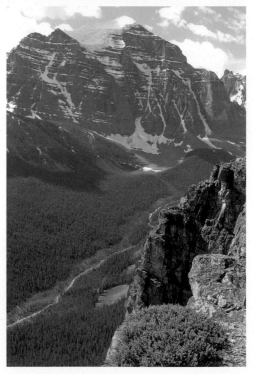

The impressive north face of Mount Temple from the summit of Saddle Mountain. Lake Annette is the one bright spot in forested Paradise Valley.

13 *Larch Valley & Sentinel Pass*

Distance 9 km return to Larch
Valley, 11.6 km to Sentinel Pass
Height gain 540 m, 725 m to pass
High point 2430 m
Moderate
Mid-July to early October

Start: Follow signs from Lake Louise Village uphill toward the lake. Turn left on Moraine Lake Road and drive 12 km to a large parking lot.

Difficulty: A wide, well-maintained trail switchbacks moderately to the relatively flat valley. Moderately graded switchbacks lead up to Sentinel Pass.

Group Access

The Moraine Lake area is often subject to access restrictions as a result of grizzly bear activity. Check at the Information Centre in Lake Louise before you head out.

Group access legally requires people entering the Moraine Lake backcountry to travel in a tight group of four or more. A tight group means that the person in the front must be able to comfortably speak with the person at the back at all times.

If you wish to hike when group access is in effect you should wait for other hikers at the trailhead and organize yourselves into a group. There is also a sign-up book outside the Lake Louise Visitor Centre.

A friendly chipmunk at Sentinel Pass. Chipmunks are smaller than golden-mantled ground squirrels (page 12) and have more stripes.

A premier Canadian Rockies experience. Feathery larches—gold in the fall—tranquil tarns, eroded pinnacles and outstanding views.

1. Walk past the lodge to a trailhead sign and turn right. Climb through spruce and fir forest in a series of moderate switchbacks with improving views. At the top of the switchbacks you arrive at a junction with a welcome seat. Eiffel Lake is straight on. Bear right—no pun intended.

2. After a few minutes you enter Larch Valley and see the first stands of larches. The trail begins to swing right and climbs gently up a series of benches to the open upper valley. The imposing mass of Mount Temple is ahead to the right. To the left is Pinnacle Mountain. Arrive at a small tarn, one of the several Minnestimma Lakes. This is the usual turnaround point for hikers who don't want to go on to Sentinel Pass.

However, the pass is worth visiting for the view of the pinnacles on the eroded ridge of Pinnacle Mountain and the panoramic view of the Ten Peaks.

3. From the lake the trail switchbacks up the steep slope to the pass. Head on up. It takes most people under half an hour. It is worth scrambling the short distance up to a viewpoint on the Mount Temple side of the pass.

4. Return the way you came. If group access is in effect, be sure to stay with a group all the way down.

Note: At Sentinel pass you may be tempted to ascend Mount Temple. This is a scrambling route with serious routefinding difficulties due to the many off-route trails that have appeared in recent years. Don't go unless you have scrambling and routefinding experience on big mountains.

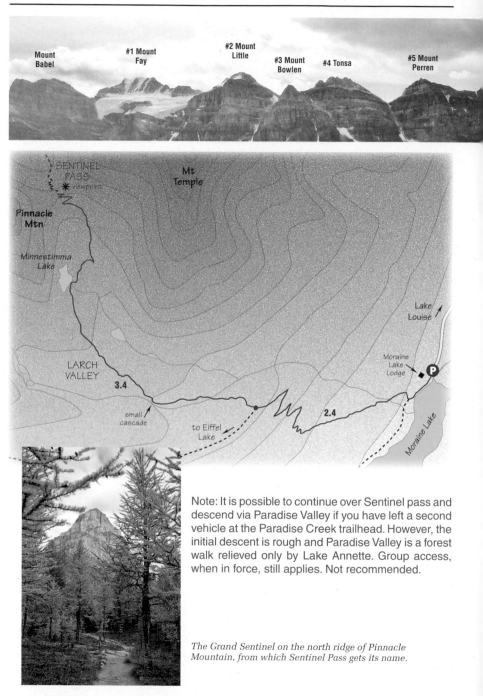

Note: It is possible to continue over Sentinel pass and descend via Paradise Valley if you have left a second vehicle at the Paradise Creek trailhead. However, the initial descent is rough and Paradise Valley is a forest walk relieved only by Lake Annette. Group access, when in force, still applies. Not recommended.

The Grand Sentinel on the north ridge of Pinnacle Mountain, from which Sentinel Pass gets its name.

#6 Mount
Allen

#7 Mount
Tuzo

#8 Deltaform
Mountain

#9 Neptuak
Mountain

Nine of the Ten Peaks. Wenkchemna Peak, though a shoulder of Mount Hungabee, is regarded as #10.

Snow-sprinkled Mounts Allen (left) and Tuzo and Deltaform Mountain provide a background for the just turning fall colours of Lyell's larches.

The upper Minnestimma Lake with Sentinel Pass in the background. The southwest face of Mount Temple is to the right.

The switchback trail to Sentinel Pass takes most people less than half an hour from the lake below.

The broken ridge of Pinnacle Mountain with Mount Lefroy in the background from the viewpoint just above the pass (3).

Looking down on the pass with Larch Valley in the background.

14 Eiffel Lake

Distance 12.6 km return
Height gain 365 m
High point 2255 m
Moderate
July to end of September

Stunning views of the Ten Peaks across an impressive moraine-filled cirque with the option to climb to a high pass.

Start: Follow signs from Lake Louise Village uphill toward the Lake. Turn left on Moraine Lake Road and drive 12 km to a large parking lot.

Difficulty: A wide, well-maintained trail that switchbacks moderately to start with, then traverses easily under the slopes of Eiffel Peak.

Note: Read the section on Group Access on page 53 before heading out on this hike.

Hoary marmot.

1. Walk past the lodge to a trailhead sign and turn right. Climb through spruce and fir forest in a series of moderate switchbacks. At the top of the switchbacks, 2.7 km from the parking lot, you arrive at a junction. Eiffel Lake is straight on.

2. The gradually ascending trail soon breaks out of the trees and traverses the lower, lightly treed open slopes of Eiffel Peak. Climb to a large boulder slope and pick your way across any lingering snow patches. Crest a slight rise and you will see Eiffel Lake below. The trail traverses a steep scree slope above the lake to a rocky promontory with larch trees and large rocks to sit on. The views of the Ten Peaks are stunning—they appear so close.

3. Return the way you came. If group access is in effect, be sure to stay with a group all the way down.

Mount Tuzo (left) and Deltaform and Neptuak mountains from the trail.

Approaching the rocky promontory (2), the usual turnaround point for those not wishing to continue to Wenkchemna Pass.

Eiffel Lake with pale green larches in the foreground.

Going farther to Wenkchemna Pass

Distance add 6.4 km return
Height gain add 330 m
High point 2611 m

Extend your hike later in the season when the snow has melted, to a high pass overlooking Prospectors Valley.

1. From the rocky promontory above Eiffel Lake the trail contours into the upper cirque of Wenkchemna Valley, switchbacking across rocky meadows to just below the pass. The old trail that swung right under the ridge of Wenkchemna Peak has been obliterated by the collapse of a rocky moraine, leaving a very unstable slope. A trail is now developing directly up moraine below the pass.

2. Turn left off the original trail at a large split boulder. After a short section of meadow, scramble up the moraine—a few cairns—to the pass.

3. It is worthwhile scrambling about 500 m up the ridge of Neptuak Mountain to a high point with cairn for an outstanding view of Opabin Pass and the head of Prospectors Valley.

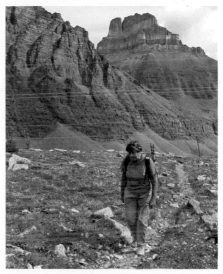

Heading up toward Wenkchemna Pass.

The approach to Wenkchemna Pass. The route heads up a shallow valley to the right of the centre of the picture, then up the steep scree directly to the pass.

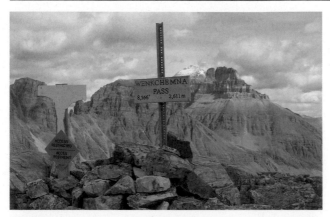

The white wooden notice on the pass has probably been chewed by a hungry porcupine.

Centre: Looking toward Neptuak Mountain. It is worth scrambling to the cairn visible on the low ridge to the right.

Mount Biddle with Opabin Pass, gateway to Lake O'Hara, to the right.

15 Yoho Lake Loop

Distance 10.4 km loop
Height gain 290 m
High point 1815 m
Fairly easy
Late June to end of September

Start: Drive the Trans-Canada Hwy. to the Yoho Valley Road, 3.6 km east of Field (the first junction to the right after the bottom of the hill if you are coming from Lake Louise). Drive the Yoho Valley Road for 13.8 km to the parking lot at Takakkaw Falls. Although the trail starts from the Whiskey Jack Hostel you can only park at the trailhead if you are staying at the hostel.

Difficulty: A good, well-graded trail with moderately steep switchbacks at the start. The Iceline portion of the trail is rocky.

1. From the southern end of Takakkaw Falls parking lot, follow the paved tourist trail toward the falls. At the bridge, continue straight on to the trailhead near the Whiskey Jack Hostel.

2. The trail switchbacks up avalanche paths to where a trail branches left to Hidden Lakes (an optional 600 m detour). Keep straight ahead and climb to a second junction to Yoho Lake. Keep left.

3. The trail makes a long, easy traverse across the hillside before climbing over a low ridge. The trail climbs easily through floral meadows and briefly alongside the creek while swinging around to the south end of Yoho Lake.

4. Continue around the lakeshore to the campground at a three-way junction. Left heads 650 m to the forest-enclosed Yoho Pass. Keep right.

5. Follow the Highline Trail which climbs moderately steeply at first. The steepness relents and you begin a long, easy, undulating traverse through forest and across

A forest-enclosed green lake with floral meadow and views of Takakkaw Falls across the Yoho Valley.

avalanche paths and scree slopes to merge with the Iceline Trail. The view across the Yoho Valley is magnificent.

6. Turn right onto the Iceline Trail (loose and rocky) and follow it down to the Yoho Lake junction (2). Keep left and return the way you came.

Takakkaw Falls, from the Highline Trail, during a period of high runoff.

61

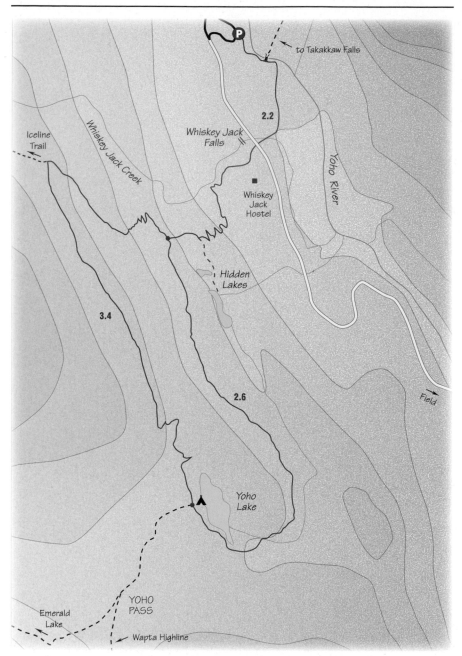

to Takakkaw Falls

2.2

Iceline
Trail

Whiskey Jack Creek

Whiskey Jack
Falls

Yoho River

Whiskey
Jack
Hostel

Hidden
Lakes

3.4

2.6

Field

Yoho
Lake

YOHO
PASS

Emerald
Lake

Wapta Highline

Yoho Lake and Wapta Mountain from near the backcountry campground.

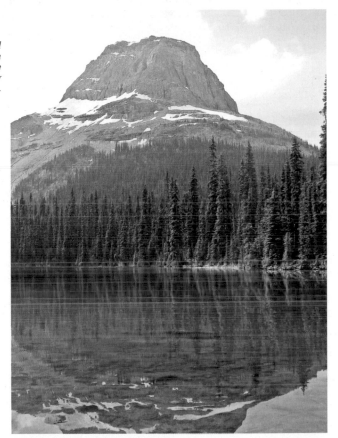

The Daly Glacier above Takakkaw Falls and the Waputik Icefield from the Highline Trail. The snow-covered peak to the left is Mount Balfour.

16 Iceline–Celeste Lake Loop

Distance 19.1 km loop
Height gain 730 m
High point 2230 m
Strenuous
Mid-July to end of September

*A high ascending traverse into
a stark land of rocky moraines,
sparkling glaciers, grey-green lakes,
tumbling waterfalls and expansive
views of snow-clad peaks.*

Start: Drive the Trans-Canada Hwy. to the Yoho Valley Road, 3.7 km east of Field (the first junction to the right after the bottom of the hill if you are coming from Lake Louise) .Drive the Yoho Valley Road for 13 km to the parking lot at Takakkaw Falls. Although the trail starts from the Whiskey Jack Hostel you may only park at the trailhead if you are staying at the hostel.

Difficulty: A good, well-graded trail that climbs high above treeline. It is best avoided in poor weather when you may wish to consider the less exposed hike #15 to Yoho Lake.

1.From the southern end of Takakkaw Falls parking lot, follow the paved tourist trail toward the falls. At the bridge, continue straight on to the trailhead near the Whiskey Jack Hostel.

2. The trail switchbacks steeply up a large avalanche path to where a trail branches left to Hidden Lake. Keep straight ahead and climb to a second junction to Yoho Lake. Turn right onto Iceline Trail.

3. Continue zigzagging upward across avalanche paths toward treeline and increasingly better views across the Yoho Valley. Arrive at a junction with the Highline Trail, which heads back to Yoho Lake. Keep straight on.

4. The trail continues to climb steadily, zigzagging to the top of a moraine where you get your first view of the sparkling Emerald Glacier, now split into two parts. The trail now heads across the slope over talus and smooth limestone slabs with occasional cairns. Cross a

creek just after a large, flat-topped rectangular rock and climb up and over the first of several lateral moraines. Meltwater from the glacier rushes down across slabs and boulders, forming a number of grey-green glacial lakes. This is the highlight of the trip. Arrive at the Celeste Lake Connector junction.

5. The high point of the trail is atop the moraine about 0.8 km away and is worth a visit. Climb the small knoll for a better view.

6. Return to the Celeste Lake Connector. You may decide to return the way you came so as to further enjoy the high alpine country. If you decide to complete the loop, turn left onto the connector.

7. The trail descends beneath moraine to a flowery alpine meadow and then into trees. Pass Celeste Lake (two lakes in low water conditions) and continue down to Little Yoho Valley. Just after Little Gem Pond, descend to the turbulent creek and cross the bridge. Turn right onto Little Yoho Valley trail at the top of the bank.

8. Pass the junction to the Whaleback after a few metres. While it is possible for strong hikers to cross the Whaleback to Twin Falls,. it makes for a long day (25.4 km and 380 m additional height gain. Continue descending to Laughing Falls and the junction with the Yoho Valley trail, passing the junction with the Marpole Connector (a strenuous hike across a rockpile) after 500 m.

9. Turn right and follow the Yoho Valley trail downhill to start with, then broad and almost flat, back to Takakkaw Falls.

The remnants of the Emerald Glacier below Michael Peak (4).

The Emerald Glacier.

Looking down from the first moraine to the creek crossing and the flat-topped boulder (4).

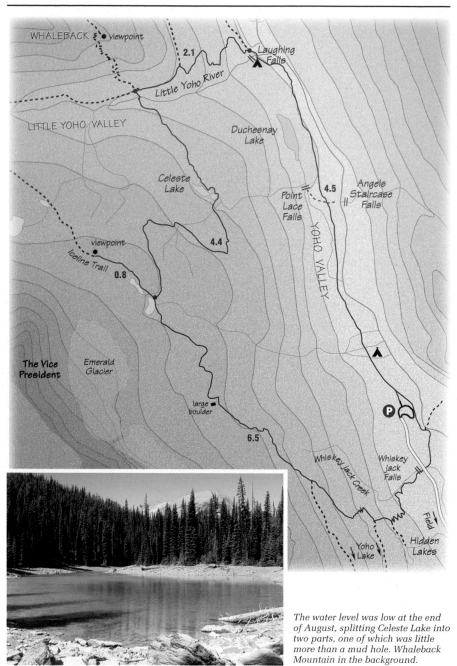

WHALEBACK • viewpoint

2.1

Laughing
Falls

Little Yoho River

LITTLE YOHO VALLEY

Duchesnay
Lake

Celeste
Lake

Point
Lace
Falls

4.5

Angels
Staircase
Falls

YOHO VALLEY

viewpoint

Iceline Trail

0.8

4.4

The Vice
President

Emerald
Glacier

large
boulder

6.5

Whiskey Jack Creek

Whiskey
Jack
Falls

P

Field

Yoho
Lake

Hidden
Lakes

The water level was low at the end
of August, splitting Celeste Lake into
two parts, one of which was little
more than a mud hole. Whaleback
Mountain in the background.

The northern portion of the Emerald Glacier under The Vice President from the Celeste Lake Connector junction (4).

Centre. Looking across barren talus toward the Little Yoho Valley from the small knoll above the high point of the trail (5). The glaciated peak is Mount McArthur with Isolated Peak to the right.

The meadows below the Iceline Trail (7) are a refreshing contrast to the stark talus slopes above.

67

17 Yoho Valley to Twin Falls

Distance 16 km return
Height gain 300 m
High point 1820 m
Moderately strenuous
July to end of September

Spectacular waterfalls, raging torrents and a teahouse, with the option of alpine meadows and a high ridge with superlative views.

Start: Drive the Trans-Canada Hwy. to the Yoho Valley Road, 3.7 km east of Field (the first junction to the right after the bottom of the hill if you are coming from Lake Louise). Drive the Yoho Valley Road for 13 km to the parking lot at Takakkaw Falls. Park in the northernmost parking area, just before the overnight parking only section.

Difficulty: A wide, almost level trail to start, then a moderate, well-graded trail through trees for the rest of the way.

1. Walk through the overnight only parking area and continue on the trail and a short section of road to the campground and a trailhead kiosk.

2. Follow the wide, almost level trail up valley across an open alluvial fan with a bridged creek. Pass a junction to viewpoints for Angels Staircase Falls (right)

and Point Lace Falls a short distance to the left. Both are worth seeing.

3. The trail becomes narrower and climbs gently to a junction with a short trail to Duchesnay Lake. Continue to Laughing Falls and the junction with Little Yoho Valley trail.

4. Continue up-valley for about 2 km through forest, crossing Twin Falls Creek to its east bank and climb steadily to a junction with Yoho Glacier Trail.

5. Keep left on the main trail and climb moderately steeply with a few switchbacks. The roar of Twin Falls becomes louder and you arrive at a junction, and a map of the area. Turn left for Twin Falls Chalet. To the right is the trail to the Whaleback.

6. After viewing the falls, and maybe having afternoon tea, return the way you came.

Twin Falls Chalet.

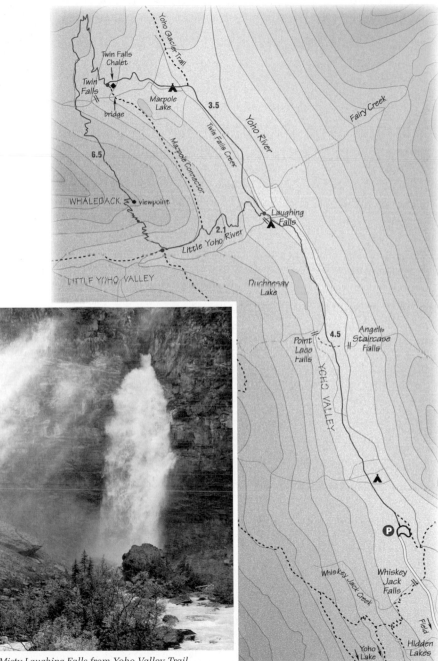

Misty Laughing Falls from Yoho Valley Trail.

Twin Falls.

Going farther to the Whaleback

Distance add 5.1 km
Height gain add 285 m

A panoramic view of the Yoho Valley is the reward for taking this strenuous alternative return route. After the initial climb and descent to the very lip of Twin Falls, there is a delightful climb through subalpine meadows to the ridgetop.

1. From Twin Falls Chalet head back the way you came a short distance to the junction with the trail down to the Yoho Valley (5). Keep straight on.

2. A good dirt trail winds up through forest to the foot of the cliffs, then climbs moderately beneath the rock walls until it is able to switchback steeply to the top. The trail then descends to emerge at the top of the cliffs near the falls. You

can head across bare rock slabs to stand on the very lip of the cascade. Take care! Scramble back to the trail and head for the bridge a short distance upstream. This is a seasonal bridge, so if hiking early in the season check at the information centre in Field to ensure that it is in place.

3. The trail now ascends subalpine meadows in a series of easy switchbacks before traversing moderately steeply to the ridgetop. A cairn marks the descent trail to the right. Go straight for 85 m to the open ridgetop and a monument to a skier killed in an avalanche in 1962. Enjoy the panoramic view.

4. Retrace your steps to the cairn and turn left, immediately beginning a long series of switchbacks 300 vertical metres down a steep gully to Little Yoho Valley trail.

5. Turn left and follow the Little Yoho Valley trail down to Laughing Falls. Turn right on the Yoho Valley trail and reach Takakkaw Falls parking in 4.5 km.

Looking back down the trail toward Twin Falls Creek (3). The triangular snow-covered peak is Mont des Poilus.

The lip of Twin Falls (2).

18 Lake Oesa & Lake O'Hara

Distance 7.2 km return
Height gain 240 m
High point 2285 m
Moderate
Mid-July to end of September

Lake O'Hara: the crown jewel of the Canadian Rockies. Blue lakes, green ponds, delicate larches, cascades and spectacular alpine views.

Start: Drive the Trans-Canada Hwy. 12.4 km west of Lake Louise and turn left onto the Lake O'Hara access road. Cross the railway tracks and immediately turn right on a gravel road which leads to the parking lots. Board the bus for Lake O'Hara if you have reservations (see page 4) or walk the access trail 11 km to the lake.

Difficulty: Good, well-graded trail around the lake with some rocky sections on the trail to Lake Oesa.

1. Get off the bus at Le Relais Day Shelter. Head across the road toward the lake, past the warden cabin, and turn left on the Lakeshore Trail. Follow it to the bridge over the outlet creek.

2. Cross the bridge and embark on the undulating trail along the north side of Lake O'Hara. Ignore the trail to Wiwaxy Gap which heads to the left after 400 m and carry on to a junction where the Lake Oesa trail leaves the Lakeshore Trail. Fork left.

3. The trail zigzags steeply to the top of a low rockband, then ascends more gradually up a series of rocky benches. Pass Yukness Lake. Ignore a junction to the right just before Victoria Lake and continue past Lefroy Lake to a high point on the trail and a four-way junction—Wiwaxy Gap and Abbot pass to the left, Yukness Ledge to the right.

A bird's-eye view of Lake O'Hara from All Souls' Alpine Route. The low peaks to the left are the Wiwaxy Peaks. In the background is Mount Huber and the long ridge of Mount Victoria.

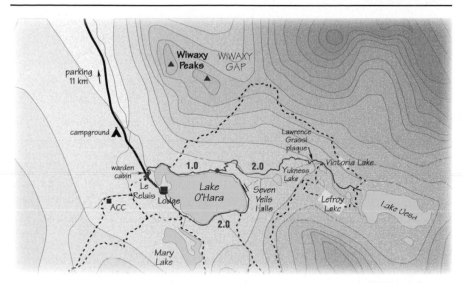

4. Pick your way down to Lake Oesa on bits of trail and over slabs for a well-deserved break.

5. Head back the way you came to Lake O'Hara. At the junction by the lake turn sharply left on Lakeshore Trail, passing below Seven Veils Falls. Arrive at the junction with the rerouted East Opabin Trail (it is shown incorrectly on most maps).

6. Continue around the lakeshore, passing the West Opabin junction and arriving at the lodge by a dock. Turn left on a short trail that skirts the lodge and comes out on the road. Walk back along the road to Le Relais.

A plaque remembering Canadian Rockies trailbuilder Lawrence Grassi.

On the way to Lake Victoria. One of the many sets of steps built by Lawrence Grassi.

73

A little way after the Lawrence Grassi plaque there is a low waterfall featured in a watercolour "Below Lake Oesa" by Walter J. Phillips, a great Canadian watercolour painter and printmaker.

Lake Victoria and Ringrose Peak.

Lefroy Lake.

Large rock slabs by the shore of Lake Oesa make a good lunch spot.

Bottom left: Mount Lefroy from the dock by the Lodge (7).

Bottom right: Columbian ground squirrel by Lefroy Lake.

19 Wiwaxy–Opabin Alpine Circuit

Distance 10.1 km loop
Height gain 600 m
High point 2532 m
Strenuous
Mid-July to end of September

A steep ascent to a high col and a traverse of narrow, exposed rocky ledges provide a spectacular high-level tour of Lake O'Hara's two main alpine valleys.

Start: Drive the Trans-Canada Hwy. 12.4 km west of Lake Louise and turn left onto the Lake O'Hara access road. Cross the railway tracks and immediately turn right on a gravel road which leads to the parking lots. Board the bus for Lake O'Hara if you have reservations (see page 4) or walk the access trail 11 km to the lake.

Difficulty: A mixture of good, well-graded trails, narrow, exposed ledges and some minor scrambling. Don't attempt this route unless the Huber Ledges are completely clear of snow.

Mount Biddle from a triple viewpoint a little way above Lake O'Hara on the trail to Wiwaxy Gap.

1. From Le Relais Day Shelter head toward the lake, past the warden cabin, and turn left on Lakeshore Trail. Follow it across the bridge over the outlet creek and continue for about 300 m to the Wiwaxy Gap trail.

2. Turn left and head up innumerable switchbacks through forest and across scree slopes with the occasional respite but increasingly better views. Finally a few turns across open scree bring you to Wiwaxy Gap.

3. Take a moment to view the next leg of your route, the Huber Ledges. It's easier than it looks. Head toward the mountain and shortly make a steep descent to the start of the ledges which are followed in a descending traverse with magnificent views across the face of Mount Huber to just above Lake Oesa. A steep descent brings you to the junction with the Lake Oesa trail about 200 m from the lake.

4. Pick your way down to Lake Oesa on bits of trail and over slabs for a well-deserved break.

5. Back at the junction head south on the Yukness Ledge trail. It initially angles toward the lake before dropping down to ford the outlet stream.

Watch for paint marks on the rocks indicating the best route. If the going becomes difficult or exposed you are off route.

6. The trail climbs gradually over rocks and slabs before making a sudden descent to meet up with the shortcut trail from Victoria Lake. Turn left.

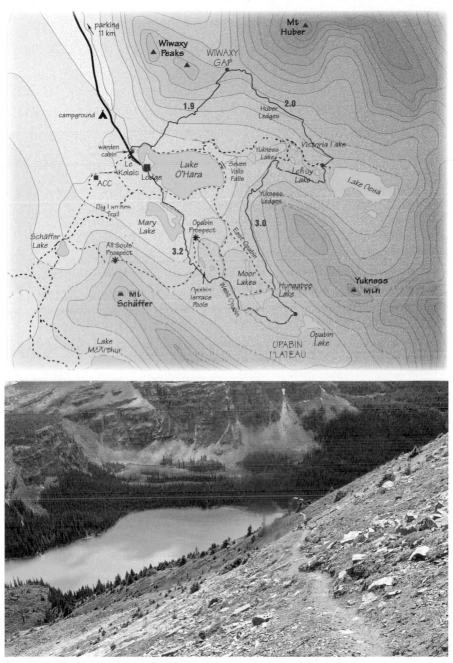

The trail up to Wiwaxy Gap from Lake O'Hara.

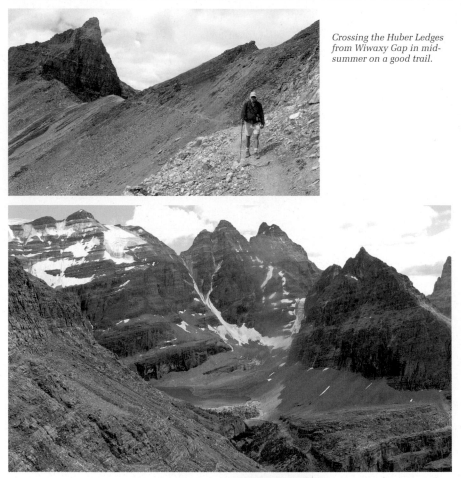

Crossing the Huber Ledges from Wiwaxy Gap in mid-summer on a good trail.

Centre: Rounding the corner toward Lake Oesa. At bottom right, the trail can be seen heading across slabby ground before turning rightward across the Yukness Ledges. From left to right are Mount Lefroy, Glacier Peak, Ringrose Peak and Yukness Mountain.

A narrow section of the Yukness Ledges trail.

Opabin Lake with Opabin Glacier and Pass to the right.

7. The route now follows a series of terraces and ledges, changing levels occasionally as it traverses across the lower slopes of Yukness Mountain toward Opabin Plateau. The ledges give way to a steep boulderfield which is first traversed and then descended to meet the East Opabin Trail on the Opabin Plateau. Turn left for Opabin Lake.

There are many options here and two different routes back to Lake O'Hara (see dashed lines on map). I suggest and describe the West Opabin Trail with a visit to Opabin Prospect, a superlative viewpoint. An alternative is to retrace your steps back to the Yukness Ledge junction and carry on down East Opabin Trail to the Lake O'Hara Shoreline Trail, which can be followed either way around the lake to your starting point.

8. From Opabin Lake head southwest on the West Opabin Trail, which switchbacks down to Hungabee Lake. Continue down, ignoring the cutoff to the East Opabin Trail on the right, to a junction just before a small pond (one of the Cascade Lakes). Turn left and cross the creek.

9. If you wish to visit Opabin Prospect—well worth the effort—turn right at the next junction and follow the trail through larches to the Prospect. After admiring the tremendous view over Lake O'Hara continue on the trail past one of the Opabin Terrace Pools to the West Opabin Trail (a 750 m loop). Turn right.

10. After a few metres you will see the All Souls' Prospect trail heading off to the left. This is the trail to take if you are hiking the option (page 81). Otherwise go straight on. You now begin a fairly steep zigzag descent to Mary Lake, traversing the slope below the sheer cliffs of Opabin Prospect. Follow the trail through trees around the north side of Mary Lake to a junction.

12. Turn right for the Lake O'Hara Shoreline Trail and Lake O'Hara Lodge or left for a more scenic route via the Alpine Meadow to Le Relais or the ACC hut. For Le Relais, keep right at all junctions except the last one 50 m above the road.

One of the Cascade Lakes on an optional descent route just off the Opabin Prospect Trail.

Wiwaxy Peaks from Opabin Prospect.

Mary Lake with Lake O'Hara in the distance from West Opabin Trail.

Extend the circuit via the All Souls' Alpine Route

Distance add 1.5 km
Height gain add 285 m
High point 2475

This option is for the purist who wants to do the complete Alpine Route. It is a demanding uphill to a superb viewpoint followed by a steep rocky descent to Schäffer Lake.

1. After descending from Opabin Plateau pass both junctions to Opabin Prospect and, shortly after the second one, turn left on All Souls' route (10). The rocky trail climbs moderately at first, then more steeply and at the end of the day seems more than 285 m. The reward is the marvellous view across Lake O'Hara to Wiwaxy Peak and Mount Huber.

2. It's all downhill from the Prospect, very steep, loose and rocky. Carry on across the ridge, following cairns, paint marks and sections of trail steeply

downhill on the west side of the ridge to a junction with Big Larches Trail just before Schäffer Lake. Big Larches Trail is rocky, rooty and involves extra height gain. Not recommended.

3. Turn left and arrive at beautiful Schäffer Lake in 100 m. Turn right at the junction by the lake to return to Lake O'Hara via the ACC hut. Carry on past the hut, keep left at a junction and cross the ridge to Le Relais.

All Souls' Prospect.

A cold September day on the All Souls' Alpine Route. Mounts Ringrose and Hungabee in the cloud.

20 Lake McArthur

A blue glacial lake with an impressive mountain backdrop, tranquil tarns and larch forest.

Distance 7 km return
Height gain 230 m
High point 2320 m
Fairly easy
July to end of September

Start: Drive the Trans-Canada Hwy. 12.4 km west of Lake Louise and turn left onto the Lake O'Hara access road. Cross the railway tracks and turn immediately right on a gravel road which is followed to the parking lots. Board the bus for Lake O'Hara if you have reservations (see page 4) or walk the access trail 11 km to the lake.

Difficulty: An good, well-graded trail with moderate height gain.

1. From Le Relais, follow the trail that leads away from the lake over a low ridge to Alpine Meadows. Continue past the ACC's Elizabeth Parker hut and bear left up a forested draw. The trail zigzags up through forest to Schäffer Lake.

2. Cross the bridge over the outlet stream and carry on around the lake to a junction with McArthur Pass Trail.

3. Keep left on the High-Level Trail, which at first follows the shoreline of Schäffer Lake, then climbs along the base of a rocky slope in open larch forest to a junction with Odaray Highline Trail. Keep straight on.

4. After 200 m there is another junction that marks the diversion of the Low-Level and High-Level trails. Keep straight on the High-Level Trail. Continue climbing toward a cliffband which is easily negotiated with some scrambling.

5. The trail moderates above the cliffband and climbs to a ridge with a cairn overlooking Lake McArthur. Descend easily to the lake, ignoring various side trails. At the lake, a side trail to the left leads to a rocky vantage point.

Schäffer Lake with Mount Huber and Wiwaxy Peaks hazy due to smoke from forest fires.

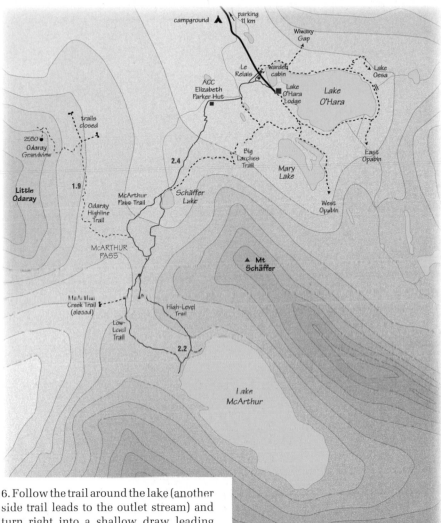

6. Follow the trail around the lake (another side trail leads to the outlet stream) and turn right into a shallow draw leading down the valley. Crest a slight rise and follow the trail past a small tarn (McArthur Pool) to the treed valley and the junction with McArthur Creek Trail.

7. Keep right and soon reach your ascent trail. Turn left. The Odaray Highline junction is reached in 200 m. Turn left, then right at the next junction onto McArthur Pass Trail, which leads back to Schäffer Lake.

8. Turn left at Schäffer Lake and retrace your ascending route back to Lake O'Hara.

Big Larches Trail is an alternative way back from Schäffer Lake, however it is rocky, rooty, involves extra height gain and is not recommended.

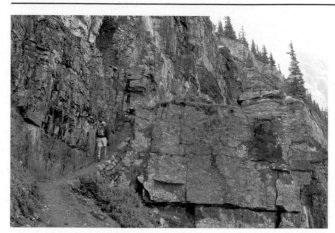

Approaching the easy scramble up the cliffband (4).

Opposite: Lake McArthur with Mount Biddle (left) and Park Mountain from the rocky trail up to Odaray Grandview. A little farther down the trail you get a view of the Goodsirs.

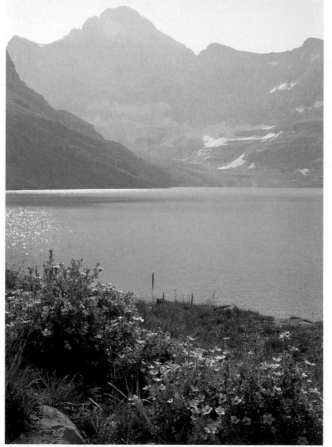

Lake McArthur with Mount Biddle in the haze. The yellow flowers in the foreground are Cinquefoil.

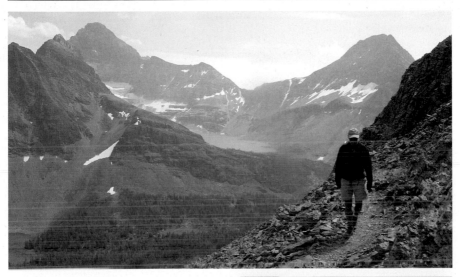

Extend your hike to Odaray Grandview

Distance add 3.8 km
Height gain add 310 m
High point 2530 m

Odaray Grandview offers a "grand view" of Lake O'Hara and the surrounding mountains. Experienced hikers will find it worthwhile, though a bit of a grunt.

Note: In the past this trail had been subject to limited access with only 3 parties a day allowed. At the time of writing this has been discontinued, but may be re implemented if the bear situation warrants.

Remnants of glacier on Mount Odaray seen from Odaray Grandview

1. On your return from Lake McArthur, instead of turning right onto McArthur Pass Trail (6) keep straight on Odaray Highline. The trail climbs gently through flower meadows then contours across the lower slopes of Little Odaray to a four-way junction. Two of the trails are closed, so your only option is to turn left onto the alpine route to Odaray Grandview.

2. The trail, marked with blue and yellow rectangles, climbs moderately at first into a small rock-strewn bowl, then more steeply up and around cliffbands and along rocky ledges, finally emerging on the edge of a plateau at a small cairn. There are two alternatives here: up and to the right gives a close up view of the small glacier on Mount Odaray, while to the left and up brings you to the large Grandview cairn. Enjoy the view—you've earned it.

3. Return the way you came, turning left onto McArthur Pass Trail to take you back to Schäffer Lake.

21 *Emerald Lake Circuit*

A superb short, scenic nature walk around an "Emerald" lake with varied views and changing vegetation.

Distance 5.4 km loop
Height gain negligible
High point 1300 m
Easy
June to end of September

Start: Drive the Trans-Canada Hwy. to Field. Head west from Field for 1.6 km to the Emerald Lake Road which is followed for 9 km to its end. The trailhead is at the far end of the parking lot.

Difficulty: Easy, well-maintained trail. Can be enjoyed in either direction. Here it is described clockwise.

1. Don't cross the bridge to the lodge. From the trailhead, head clockwise around the lake on the trail, paved to start with crossing a large avalanche path to a scenic viewpoint. Seats along the lakeshore allow you to rest and enjoy the view of shapely Mount Burgess back across the lake and Wapta Mountain (home to the Burgess Shale World Heritage site) to the east.

2. A few sections of old horse trail still exist. When in doubt choose the trail closest to the lake. Arrive at the junction with the Emerald Basin trail (see option).

3. Keep right and follow the north shore across a large alluvial fan created by the outwash from the President Range. Ignore a trail to Yoho Pass to the left. Continue to the inlet bridge, which is crossed to the east shore.

4. The trail now leads into dense, moist forest, a surprising contrast to the west and north shores. This illustrates the effect of the microclimate created by the lake and its surrounding mountains. Follow the cool, damp trail to the beginning of the south shore where it turns right and arrives at the Burgess Pass junction. Keep straight on.

Emerald Lake Lodge from the interpretive viewpoint near the start of the trail.

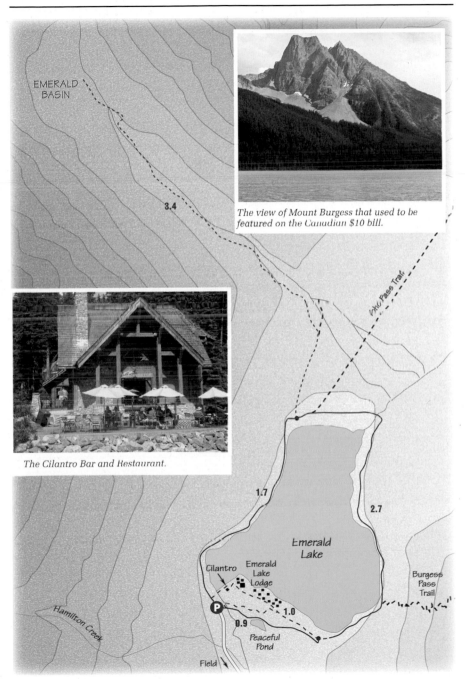

The view of Mount Burgess that used to be featured on the Canadian $10 bill.

The Cilantro Bar and Restaurant.

EMERALD BASIN

3.4

Yoho Pass Trail

1.7

2.7

Emerald Lake

Cilantro

Emerald Lake Lodge

Burgess Pass Trail

P

0.9

1.0

Hamilton Creek

Peaceful Pond

Field

87

5. After about 500 m you reach a junction where the trail to Peaceful Pond branches off to the left. It provides the shortest way back to the parking lot and avoids the lodge complex. You can, if you wish, continue straight on skirting behind the lodge and across the bridge to your starting point.

Immediately on the lodge side of the bridge is Cilantro, a bar and restaurant open from 11:00 a.m. to 9:00 p.m. mid-June to mid-September. There is a concession window where you can purchase soft drinks and snacks.

The trail across the flats at the head of the lake. Wapta Mountain in the background.

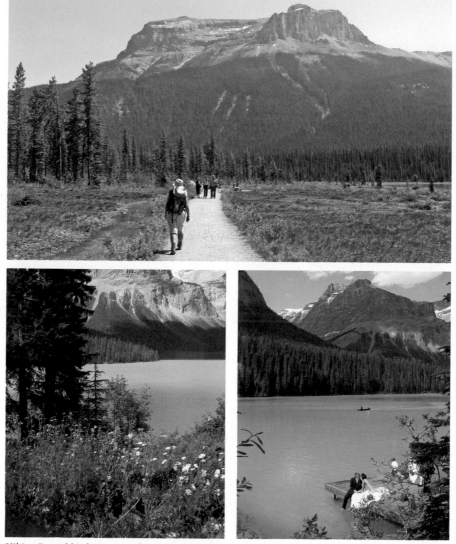

Hiking Emerald Lake is certainly not a wilderness experience. There are many activities other than hiking to entertain you and lots of photographic opportunities.

Going farther to Emerald Basin

Distance: add 6.6 km to hike around lake
Height gain 225 m
High point 1540 m

This moderately steep trail leads to an enclosed, avalanche-swept basin beneath The President and Vice President.

1. From the junction at the north end of Emerald Lake (2) the trail heads up a lightly treed gravel slope to a junction. Turn left. The trail to the right is an old horse trail which soon becomes washed out.

2. Climb moderately to start with up a rocky trail through the forest. The trail then descends slightly through trees and emerges into the open valley. Cross a large avalanche path to meet the creek.

3. Cross a small side creek (dry later in the season) and follow a good trail to the left that heads toward the twin waterfalls. The trail crosses open talus slopes before petering out among the rocks below the falls.

4. Return the way you came.

The entrance to Emerald Basin. This high cirque is ringed by Emerald Peak, Mount Carnarvon, Mount Marpole (seen above), The President and Vice President and Michael Peak.

Twin waterfalls drain the high cirque below Mount Carnarvon.

22 *Emerald Triangle*

Distance 20.3 km loop
Height gain 880 m
High point 2180 m
Very strenuous
Mid-July to mid-September

Western red cedar forest, spectacular views down to Emerald Lake and across to the President Range. Mountain goats.

Start: Drive the Trans-Canada Hwy. to Field. Head west from Field for 1.6 km to the Emerald Lake Road and follow it for 9 km to its end. Park at the near end of the parking lot and look for an unsigned trail that leads down some steps to the right (east).

Difficulty: Moderately steep, rocky on the Yoho Pass Trail. This is a strenuous outing for fit hikers. The legs of the triangle are Burgess Pass Trail, Wapta Highline Trail and Yoho Pass Trail.

out into the open on the slopes of Wapta Mountain. Here it turns north and contours across rocky alpine slopes passing two junctions to the Burgess Shale (see note below).

1. Head down the steps and across a bridge. Keep on the main trail at a junction shortly after the bridge and hike past Peaceful Pond to meet the Shoreline Trail. Turn right and continue for about 500 m to the Burgess Pass Trail—where the lakeshore trail turns left along the east shore of the lake.

2. Turn right and immediately begin the relentless climb through thick forest of spruce, pine and western red cedar. The only consolation: it's cool on a hot day, the grade is moderate and you are getting the worst of the climb over. You finally emerge on an open ridge with views of Mount Burgess and down to Emerald Lake.

3. Continue climbing to where the trail forks. To the right is the junction with the trail from Field. Keep climbing here to an excellent viewpoint, then descend to rejoin the official trail a few metres below. To avoid the climb you can head right to the junction, turn left and contour around on the main trail.

4. Turn left (east) on the Wapta Highline trail which descends slightly to the lowest point of the pass in trees, finally breaking

The trail finally emerges from thick forest. The steep north face of Mount Burgess in profile (2).

Note: On the Wapta Highline section of this trail you will pass a couple of signs advising you that the World Heritage Burgess Shale Beds are closed to the public. Don't be tempted to sneak in—the fines are high. If you wish to visit them you will need to take a tour guided by Yoho-Burgess Shale Foundation guides, 1-800-343-3006, www.burgess-shale.bc.ca/hikes.php.

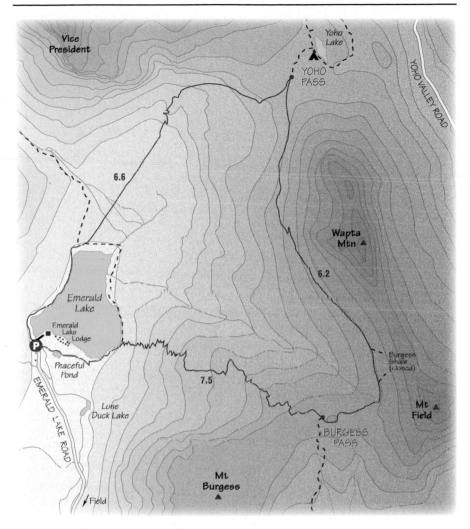

5. Just after crossing a rockslide below Wapta Mountain the trail descends in a couple of switchbacks, then traverses across five avalanche paths, the last one below a rock wall, before dropping into the forest to the junction at Yoho Pass.

Picturesque Yoho Lake is only 650 m along the trail to the right and worth a visit if you have not been there before. See trail #15.

6. From the junction head west toward Emerald Lake. The rough, rocky trail descends steeply across open slopes and rockfall to the head of the alluvial fan at the head of Emerald Lake. Hike down the gravel trail through sparse trees for almost 2 km to a junction just before the lake.

7. Turn right and follow the west shore of the lake back to the parking lot, ignoring all trails to the right.

Heading north across the open slopes of Mount Field toward Wapta Mountain (4). The Burgess Shales are up to the right.

A Yoho-Burgess Shale Foundation guided group at the rockslide (5). The President Group in the background.

Creeping Beardtongue, often called Purple Penstemon, grows profusely among the shale by the side of the trail.

Looking down to Emerald Lake from the rockslide (5).

Descending from Yoho Pass below waterfalls cascading down the steep wall of Michael Peak.

The trails around here are not always bare and dry. Crossing the alluvial fan toward the lake (6).

23 Bow Glacier Falls

Distance 9.6 km
Height gain 135 m
High point 2080 m
Fairly easy
July to end of September

A 120-m-high waterfall in a rocky glacial basin with the option of experiencing the Wapta Icefield's high mountain realm of rock and ice.

Start: Drive the Icefield Parkway north from the Trans-Canada Hwy. for 36 km to Num-ti-jah Lodge. The trailhead parking area is on the left side of the access road by public washrooms before you reach the lodge.

Difficulty: Well-trodden trail, flat for most of the way though occasionally under water, when an alternate, higher trail is available. The final section is across talus.

1. Ignore the trail by the trailhead kiosk and continue down the road past the lodge and a signed trailhead on the left side of the parking area.

2. Cross the inlet stream and follow the trail along the north shore to the gravel flats at the southwest corner of the lake. Depend-ing on water levels, you can either hike across the flats (cairns) or follow a gently undulating trail on higher ground to the right. Arrive at the beginning of a canyon.

3. The trail now climbs steeply up some steps to the rim of the canyon and a junction below which a large limestone boulder bridges the gorge. The trail to Bow Hut (see option) crosses this boulder. Keep right and continue climbing to the crest of a terminal moraine and a good view of the falls.

4. Descend into the basin and hike across talus to the base of the falls.

5. Return the way you came.

Looking across Bow Lake to the gravel flats leading up toward the falls. Sharply pointed St. Nicholas Peak on the right.

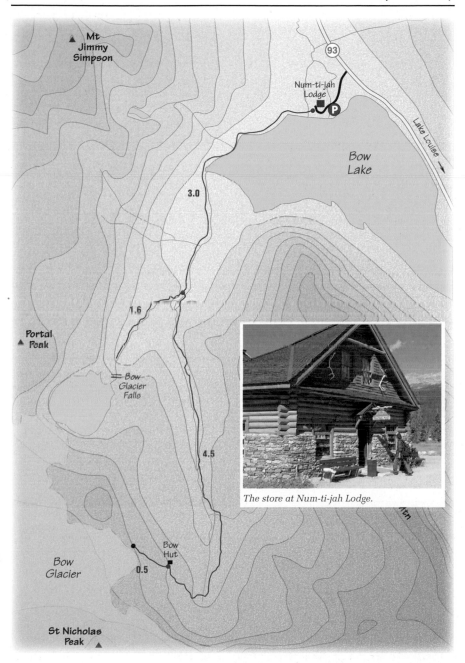

The store at Num-ti-jah Lodge.

Heading along the shoreline of Bow Lake. The umbrella can only be protection from the sun on this virtually cloudless day.

Because of its north-facing aspect and the surrounding high cliffs, Bow Glacier Falls gets little sunlight.

A group of hikers gets close up to the thundering cascade of the lower part of the falls.

Going farther to Bow Hut

Distance 15.4 km return to hut
Height gain 475 m
High point 2420 m

More of an alternative than an option. The Alpine Club of Canada's Bow Hut, one of the largest of the high mountain huts, is located just below a spur of the Wapta Icefield beneath St. Nicholas Peak. If you wish to stay at the Bow Hut, contact The Alpine Club of Canada at 403-678-3200, www.alpineclubofcanada.ca.

1. Cross the chockstone (3) where the trail to Bow Glacier Falls branches right. There is one high step-up on a small foothold initially, then a few feet of scrambling onto the broad top.

2. Follow a well-trodden path to the right. It leads up through trees, then drops down to the creek. Continue upstream ascending a steep rockslide at the resumption of the canyon to the canyon edge. The trail continues through trees and across talus near the edge of the canyon. At the end of the canyon climb steeply into a high cirque with steep cliffs at its head. You can see the hut at the top of the cliffs opposite.

3. Near the head of the cirque the trail heads right, crosses several streams and heads for the right-hand side of a gap in the cliffs. Follow cairns marking a discernible trail across this section. Zigzag up steep moraine to a shallow upper valley. Bow Hut is located near the upper right-hand edge of the valley at the top of steep cliffs.

4. Follow a trail up talus above the hut for about 500 m for a view of the small glacier under St. Nicholas Peak that allows mountaineering access to the Wapta Icefield above. This is a popular area for winter ski mountaineering.

5. Return the way you came.

Left: Scrambling over the chockstone (O1).

*Right: The canyon leading up
to the cirque below Mount Olive.*

Bow Hut, and its interior kept in immaculate condition while occupied by a climbing school.

St. Nicholas Peak and the bare ice (mid-August) of the small glacier leading up to the Wapta Icefield.

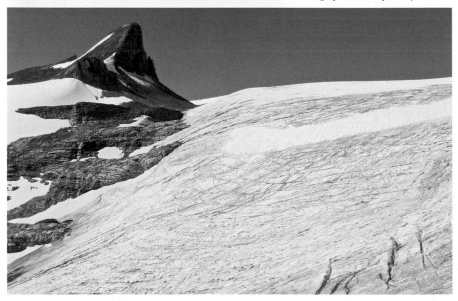

24 Helen Lake

Distance 13.8 km to ridge above lake
Height gain 570 m
High point 2520 m
Moderately strenuous
July to end of September

Easy access to flowery meadows with alpine lakes, stunning views, Hoary marmots and an easy peak for the more energetic.

Start: Icefields Parkway 33 km north of the Trans-Canada Hwy. at Lake Louise and 7.7 km south of Bow Summit. Trailhead parking is on the east side of the road opposite Crowfoot Glacier viewpoint.

Difficulty: A well-graded trail, moderately steep in places. The ascent of Cirque Peak is a non-technical scramble up scree with one easily negotiated rock band.

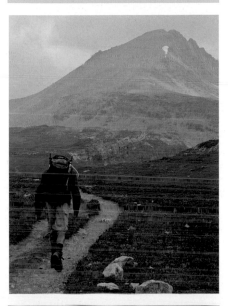

1. The trail ascends at a moderate grade through light subalpine forest then steepens as it ascends the side of an open slope and rounds the end of the ridge into more open terrain.

2. The grade eases and the trail works its way into the open subalpine cirque below Cirque Peak. Rock-hop across Helen Creek and ascend gently to Helen Lake.

3. Don't stop too long by the lake. Head for the ridge above the lake where the panoramic view is well worth the extra 125 m of height gain. Most people turn around here. If you want to extend your day see the two options on the following pages.

4. Return the way you came.

Top: The trail above Helen Creek soon after breaking out of the trees. The haze is from forest fires in British Columbia.

Bottom: Cirque Peak from Helen Lake.

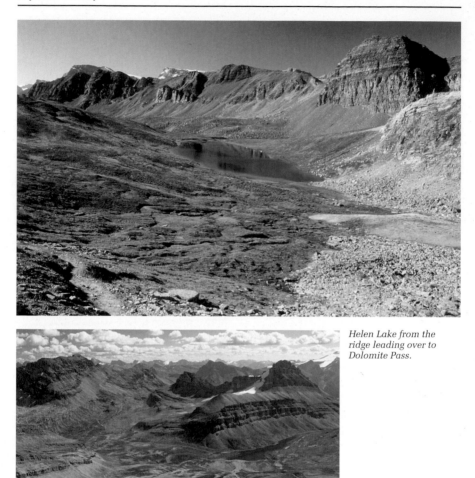

Helen Lake from the ridge leading over to Dolomite Pass.

Looking down onto the wide expanse of Dolomite Pass. Katherine Lake to the right. The other small lakes are unnamed.

Going farther to Dolomite Pass

Distance: add 5.2 km
Height gain extra 125 m to pass on return

An excursion to Katherine Lake and the barren alpine region of Dolomite Pass.

1. From the top of the ridge above Helen Lake, descend 125 m to Katherine Lake and follow the faint trail to a small lake in the environs of Dolomite Pass.

2. Return the way you came. Back up to the ridge!

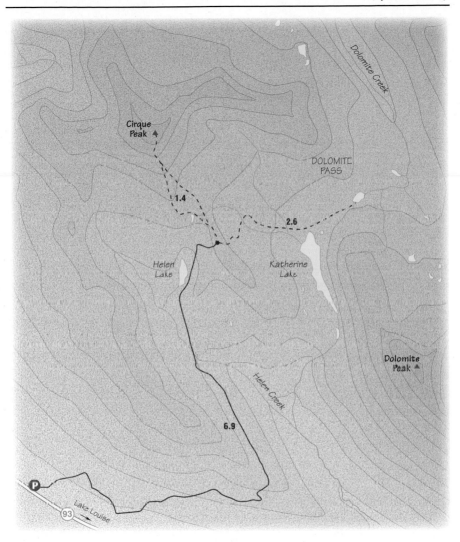

Scramble up Cirque peak

Distance: add 2.8 km to east summit
Height gain 473 m from ridge
High point 2993 m

An easy non-technical ascent to a fabulous viewpoint.

1. The route can be seen from the ridge above Helen Lake. Head across rock and scree to pick up the trail that ascends the open scree slope to the ridge or scramble onto the end of the ridge.

2. Follow the ridge to the west summit. An easy scramble will take you to the marginally higher east summit where you can sign the summit register.

3. Descend the way you came.

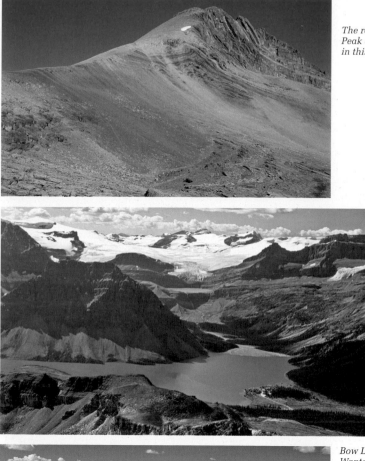

The route up Cirque Peak can be clearly seen in this picture.

Bow Lake and the Wapta Icefield from the summit of Cirque Peak.

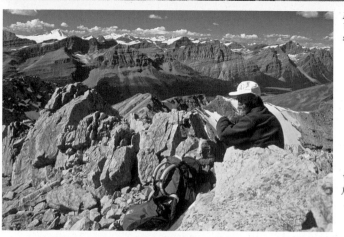

View to the south from the summit.

25 Chephren & Cirque Lakes

Distance from trailhead return:
Chephren Lake 7 km, Cirque Lake
8.4 km. Both lakes 12.8 km
Height gain 250 m (75 to Chephren)
High point 1795 m
Fairly easy
Mid-June to end of September

Start: Waterfall Lakes Campground on the Icefields Parkway 58 km north of Lake Louise and 19 km south of Saskatchewan River Crossing. If you are not camping there ignore the campground entrance and continue along the service road to a parking area on the left.

Difficulty: While there is little height gain, both trails can be wet in places. The trail to less-visited Cirque Lake is a little longer, steeper and rougher walking.

1. From the end of the parking area head straight downhill on a good track (chain across) to the trailhead by the Mistaya River bridge at the west end of the campground. The bridge is behind campsite 87.

2. Cross the bridge and ascend gradually through forest to a junction. Chephren Lake right. Cirque Lake left. The Chephren lake trail is the shorter and flatter of the two alternatives.

3. Turn right and follow the rooty trail through moderately thick forest, with a large long meadow to your left for most of

Quiet lakes below imposing peaks and steep cliffs. Worth hiking if you are staying in the campground.

the way to Chephren Lake. You are immediately below the steep east face of Mount Chephren. Howse Peak is to the left.

4. Return to the Chephren/Cirque junction and keep straight on (or turn left if heading back to the campground). Head gently downhill, make a sharp right turn, then climb to meet the outlet creek. The trail, steep in places, stays near the creek the rest of the way to the lake. At a couple of places the trail divides. Go either way. The trail ends at a large boulder field with resident marmots. The mountains that make up this impressive cirque are, from left to right, Stairway, Aries and Midway peaks. The little summit to the left is unnamed.

5. Return the way you came.

A Common Loon on Chephren Lake. It is depicted on the Canadian $1 coin—the Loonie.

Chephren Lake and Mount Chephren.

103

Cirque Lake outlet creek (4). *White Bog Orchids.*

Top: Cirque Lake below the steep cliffs of Midway Peak. The hoary marmots that inhabit the boulderfield seem unafraid of human visitors.

26 Nigel Pass

Distance 14.4 km return
Height gain 370 m
High point 2210 m
Moderate
Mid-July to mid-September

Start: The trailhead parking is along a dirt road on the east side of the Icefields Parkway 8.5 km south of the Banff-Jasper Park boundary and 0.9 km north of the Bridal Veil Falls lookout at the top of the big bend hill.

Difficulty: An easy-angled, well-graded trail until the final kilometre where it climbs 160 m moderately steeply to the pass over into the Brazeau.

Easy hiking up an open valley with scattered forest, avalanche slopes and flower-filled meadows. Views into the remote Brazeau backcountry.

1. Head down the gated access road a short distance before turning right and descending to a bridge over Nigel Creek.

2. Cross the bridge to the east side of Nigel Creek and follow the trail through light forest and across several avalanche slopes to Camp Parker a historic and prehistoric site in a large group of Engelmann spruce.

3. Ignore various side trails and continue up valley on the same side of the creek. The valley becomes more open and you pass through a succession of meadows. Arrive at a junction with a horse trail to the left.

4. Keep straight on the main trail and shortly began a moderately steep climb to the pass where a post marks the boundary between Banff and Jasper national parks.

The open valley beyond Camp Parker. The orange-coloured ridge is the head of the valley. The trail crosses a pass just left of the centre of the picture. The true Nigel Pass is to the left.

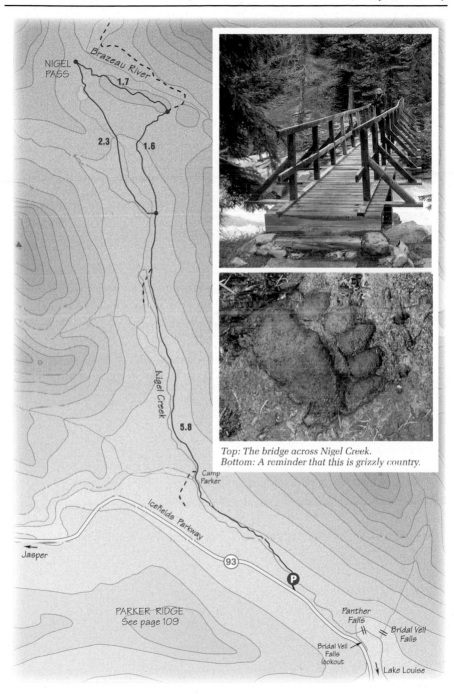

NIGEL PASS

Brazeau River

1.7

2.3 1.6

Nigel Creek

5.8

Camp Parker

Icefields Parkway

Jasper

93

P

PARKER RIDGE
See page 109

Panther Falls

Bridal Veil Falls

Bridal Veil Falls lookout

Lake Louise

Top: The bridge across Nigel Creek.
Bottom: A reminder that this is grizzly country.

107

5. Rather than continuing down the trail into the Brazeau drainage, I suggest you head left along the rocky ridge for ever improving views into the Brazeau backcountry. After 1.7 km drop down to the true Nigel Pass (it's the farthest of the two possible passes) where you will find a rarely used horse trail.

Hiking the rocky ridge above the Brazeau River.

6. Head south on the trail past a small lake, cross back into Banff National Park and continue down to the outlet creek from the lake. Cross the creek and follow the trail down-valley to the main creek. Head left on the true left side of the main creek, recross the small creek and scramble up the bank to rejoin your ascent trail.

7. Return the way you came.

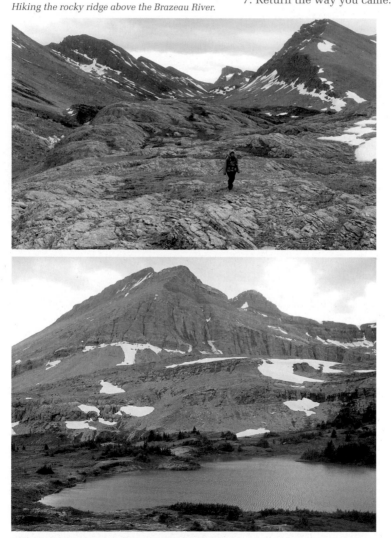

The small lake on your return route from Nigel Pass.

27 Parker Ridge

Distance 6.6 km return
Height gain 280 m
High point 2280 m
Fairly easy
Mid-July to mid-September

A good, short trail to stretch your legs when driving the Icefields Parkway. Spectacular bird's-eye view into the vastness of the Columbia Icefields.

Start: Parker Ridge is halfway along the Icefields Parkway between Lake Louise and Jasper. The trailhead—on the west side of the road—4.2 km south of the Banff-Jasper Park boundary and 5.2 km north of the Bridal Veil Falls lookout at the top of the big bend hill.

Difficulty: A fairly easy, well-maintained trail that switchbacks up to a ridge over-looking the Saskatchewan Glacier valley.

Note: Because of heavy use and delicate alpine terrain, Parks Canada closes this trail until it is dry enough for hiking. If you wish to hike it before mid-July check with the information centre in Banff or Jasper to make sure the trail is open.

1. From the parking area head upward through light forest of Engelmann spruce and subalpine fir, switchbacking to treeline in about a kilometre. Cross a large talus slope and continue switchbacking to the crest of the ridge.

2. The official trail veers left and descends from the saddle before petering out on the side of the ridge with good views of Castleguard Mountain and the rapidly receding Saskatchewan Glacier.

3. Return to the saddle and climb to a broad knoll with a couple of rock wind shelters and good views to the north and northwest. If you need exercise it is possible to continue up the ridge to a smaller knoll.

4. Return the way you came.

Hikers descending the lower section of the trail.
The peak in the background is an unnamed point on a ridge of Mount Athabasca.

The Saskatchewan Glacier leading up to the Columbia Icefield. Castleguard Mountain in the distance.

The small knoll behind the figures can be climbed for more expansive views.

28 *Wilcox Pass & Wilcox Peak Ridge*

Distance 10.8 km return
Height gain 560 m
High point 2600 m
Moderately strenuous
Mid-July to mid-September

High alpine meadows, Bighorn Sheep, snow-covered Mount Athabasca and a panoramic view of some of the highest glaciated peaks in the Canadian Rockies.

Start: Drive 108 km south of Jasper on Icefields Parkway (3.2 km south of the Icefield Centre) or 123 km north of Lake Louise. Turn east into Wilcox Creek Campground entrance road and park on the left after a few metres. For hikers staying at the Columbia Icefield Campground, there is a steep unofficial trail leading to the ridge (1) from walk in site #7.

Difficulty: Good trail, steep in a few places early on. Snow-covered most of June and usually wet until the end of July.

1. From the parking lot follow the steep trail through mature Engleman spruce and subalpine fir, breaking out of the trees for good after 1.5 km onto an open ridge with superb views of Mount Athabasca and the Athabasca Glacier.

2. Continuing uphill the trail climbs moderately steeply by Wilcox Creek before reaching the alpine tundra of the pass. A large pile of rocks with a sign marks the official summit. The actual summit is about 800–900 m farther.

3. Look for a narrow trail just beyond the official summit heading left toward the ridge. Climb over a bump and up to the edge of the broad ridge (about 1.1 km and 240 m height gain). Revel in the panoramic view of Mount Athabasca and the Columbia Icefield.

4. Return the way you came.

Approaching Wilcox Pass.
Mount Wilcox in the background.

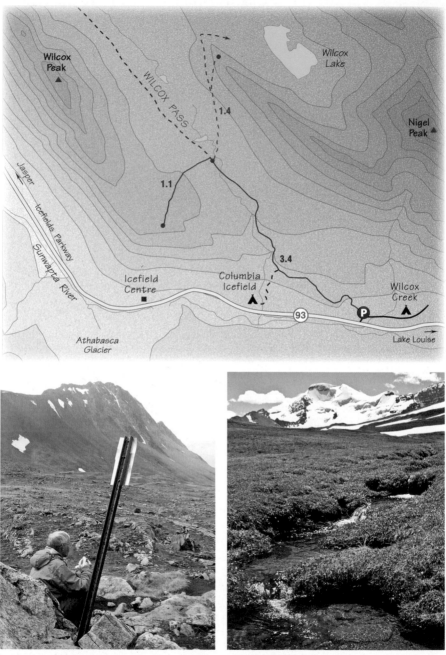

The official summit of the pass is marked with a cairn on top of a pile of rocks.

The north face of Mount Athabasca from the meadows of Wilcox Pass.

The gleaming north face of Mount Athabasca from Wilcox Peak Ridge.

Rocky Mountain Bighorn Sheep are often seen on the slopes around Wilcox Pass.

Centre: A rainy day near the summit of Wilcox Pass.

The toe of the Athabasca Glacier from Wilcox Peak Ridge in 1974. Compare it with what you see today to see how fast the glacier is receding.

113

Going farther to Wilcox Lake

Distance 1 km from pass
Height gain 120 m
High point 2515 m

This option will take you to a viewpoint for an isolated lake beneath the west face of Nigel Peak. It is possible to traverse into this remote cirque to explore the environs of the lake.

1. From the marker at the top of the pass head northeast toward the northwest ridge of Nigel Peak, staying on higher ground to avoid the bog. Contour up and across the slopes of the northwest ridge of Nigel Peak and look for a good trail heading up and across steep talus to the ridge. From here, the sloping basin with Wilcox Lake at its head is laid out before you.

If you would like to explore the basin, head farther to the northwest to a lower col, reached by a steep rock and scree

slope. As you cannot see the lake from here, you may wish to climb a little way up the ridge to a cairn. It is easy to traverse into the cirque from here.

2. Return the way you came.

Wilcox Lake is situated in a remote and fascinating high alpine valley with slabby rocks, little pools, high alpine plants, colourful lichen (top) and interesting features such as patterned ground (right).

29 *Geraldine Lakes*

Distance 10.5 km to second lake
Height gain 405 m to second lake
High point 1890 m
Moderately strenuous
July to mid-September

Picas and marmots abound in the boulderfields of this long valley with tranquil lakes, rushing cascades and high alpine cirques.

Start: From Jasper, drive south on the Icefields Parkway (Hwy. 93) for 30 km to Hwy. 93A junction at Athabasca Falls. Follow Hwy. 93A for 1.2 km to Geraldine Lake Fire Road, then 5.4 km to the end of the narrow, bumpy road.

Difficulty: Easy to first lake, then steep hills, rough, muddy, rooty, loose rocks and boulders—slippery when wet. This trail is for strong hikers. Take your time and consider turning back from Second Geraldine Lake if conditions are bad.

1. From the trailhead kiosk the trail heads up moderately steeply followed by an easy downhill to First Geraldine Lake.

2. The usually muddy path heads around the west shore to a waterfall at the end of the lake and the end of the good trail.

3. Follow an obvious path through rocks and scramble steeply up the right side of the waterfall for about 90 vertical metres emerging onto a rocky bench.

4. Angle left to the southeast side of the valley—small cairns may mark the way. Relocate the path, which soon disappears at another talus field. Look for yellow markers. Cross the creek, skirt the edge of a small pond on rocks and relocate the trail in the trees. The trail leaves the trees and crosses open rocky terrain, coming close to a second waterfall.

First Geraldine Lake. The mountain is a subsidiary peak on the north ridge of Mount Fryatt.

The waterfall by the trail (3).

The second waterfall, above the rocky bench (4).

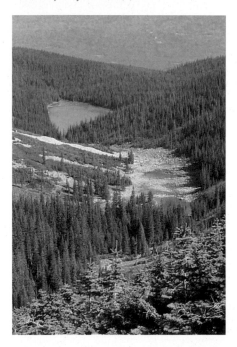

5. The trail then climbs very steeply up a gully to the left of the waterfall on dirt and loose rocks for about 100 vertical metres to the top of the headwall.

6. Continue less steeply up a talus slope to the crest of a ridge overlooking Second Geraldine Lake. Descend easily about 60 m to the lake by some trees. For many this will be the end of the trail.

7. If you are heading for the campground at the end of Second Geraldine Lake follow the trail around the east shore, rock-hopping across several boulderfields. The campground is across the creek (bridge near outlet) 6.1 km from the trailhead.

8. Return the way you came.

Shortly after you reach the top of the headwall above First Geraldine Lake you arrive at a rocky area with intermittent ponds. Head to your left (right in this picture) and pick the easiest line close to the ponds. The trail becomes obvious again at the far end of the larger pond.

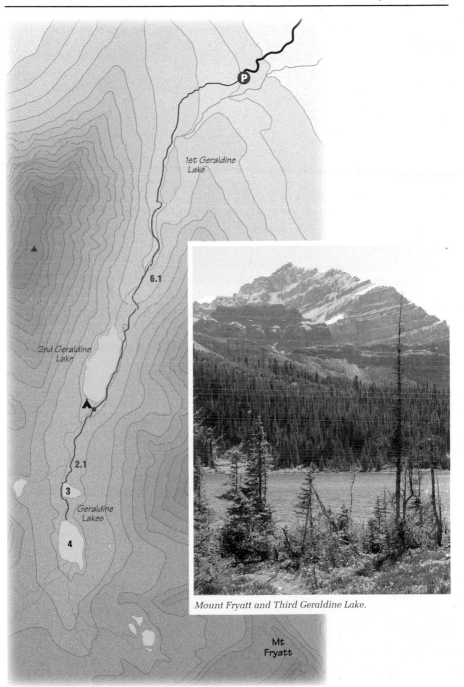

1st Geraldine Lake

6.1

2nd Geraldine Lake

2.1

3

Geraldine Lakes

4

Mt Fryatt

Mount Fryatt and Third Geraldine Lake.

Second Geraldine Lake, the largest of the four lakes, and the usual turnaround point.

Going farther to Third and Fourth Geraldine lakes.

Distance 2.1 km to Fourth Lake
Height gain 80 m to Fourth Lake
High point 1980 m

Strong hikers will want to continue to Fourth Geraldine Lake. It is a bit of a struggle getting to Third Lake through bush and across boulderfields, but once there you are in more open country near the head of the valley.

1. Continue on the east side of the creek across from the campground and follow a good but rough trail marked by cairns in places to Third Geraldine Lake.

2. Cross the creek just below the outlet to the west shore of Third Lake and follow a trail along the shore and through meadows to Fourth Geraldine Lake.

3. Return the way you came.

You finally break out into the alpine at Fourth Geraldine Lake. There is a high alpine cirque with several small lakes under the west face of Mount Fryatt that would be well worth exploring,

30 Cavell Meadows

Distance 8.3 km for all trails
Height gain 370 m
High point 2288 m
Moderate
No dogs
Road open mid-June to mid-October, but see note below

Start: From Jasper, drive south on the Icefields Parkway (Hwy. 93) for 6.7 km to Hwy. 93A junction. Follow Hwy. 93A for 5.2 km to Mount Edith Cavell Road. The narrow, winding road (drop-off area for trailers at the start) ends after 13.8 km at Edith Cavell parking lot.

Difficulty: A very popular, well-graded, moderately steep trail. Arrive early to beat the crowds and get the best lighting on the Angel Glacier.

Note: Because of heavy use and delicate alpine terrain, Parks Canada closes this trail until it is dry enough for hiking. If you wish to hike it before mid-July check with the information centre in Jasper to make sure the trail is open.

1. From either exit from the parking lot follow Path of the Glacier Trail to a junction where it continues straight on.

2. Turn left onto Cavell Meadows Trail, which switchbacks over and along the foot of a lateral moraine. Continue steeply through subalpine forest to a junction at 2.1 km. This is the start of the circuit trail.

3. Keep straight on. The trail soon arrives at the meadows with good views of Mount Edith Cavell and the Angel Glacier. At the southern end of the meadows there is a fork in the trail.

4. Turn right onto a 100 m spur trail to a viewpoint.

5. Return to the main trail and continue on it for 240 m to another junction. Keep

Flowery alpine meadows from mid-July to mid-August, the towering north face of Mount Edith Cavell and the Angel Glacier.

right. The trail to the left is a short-cut trail offering an abbreviated circuit.

6. Continue to another junction. The trail to the right climbs to a superb viewpoint on a ridge above the meadows (0.5 km distance and 100 m height gain).

7. Return to the main trail, which descends to the junction at the start of the circuit (2).

8. Descend your upcoming route to the junction with Path of the Glacier Trail (1). Turn left uphill, then descend to Cavell Pond with its miniature glacier and icebergs. Follow The Path of the Glacier back to the parking lot.

This hoary marmot seems to enjoy the attention of the crowd from among the boulders at the foot of the lateral moraine (2).

Hiking up by the lateral moraine (2). The marmot on the previous page was photographed here.

The Angel Glacier on the north face of Mount Edith Cavell from the trail at (7).

Heading up toward the high point (6). Unfortunately the cloud was rolling in.

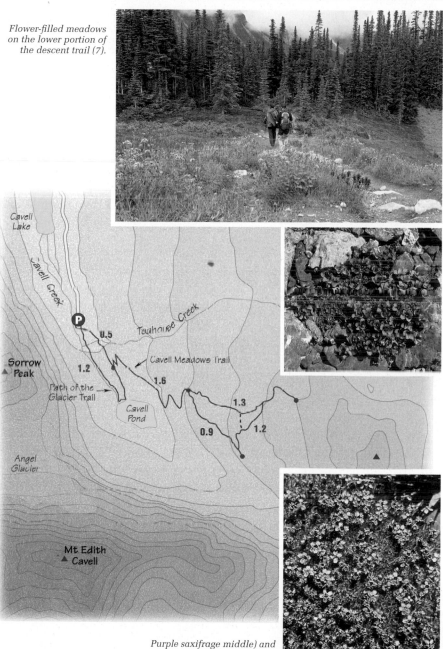

Flower-filled meadows on the lower portion of the descent trail (7).

Cavell Lake

Cavell Creek

Teahouse Creek

P

0.5

Sorrow Peak

1.2

Path of the Glacier Trail

Cavell Meadows Trail

1.6

Cavell Pond

1.3

0.9

1.2

Angel Glacier

Mt Edith Cavell

Purple saxifrage middle) and moss campion are found at higher elevations on this trail.

121

Descending the side of the moraine toward Cavell Pond. Note the small remnant glacier that breaks apart to produce the icebergs.

Icebergs in Cavell Pond on Path of the Glacier Trail (8).

31 Valley of the Five Lakes

Distance 6.4 km
Height gain 105 m
High point 1135 m
Easy
Mid-May to end of October

Clear, blue-green lakes of varied hue in a forest setting. A popular family outing as well as a good destination during inclement weather.

Start: From Jasper, drive south on the Icefields Parkway (Hwy. 93) for 8.8 km to a parking lot on the east side shortly after the bridge over the Athabasca River.

Difficulty: A very popular, well graded trail. These trails are part of the Jasper numbered trails system. You will be following trails #9a and #9b. Some sections of trail are heavily used by cyclists.

1. From the parking lot follow the trail through lodgepole pine and across the boardwalk protecting Wabasso Creek wetlands. Arrive at a four-way junction (trail #9). Left leads, in about 8 km, to Old Fort Point near Jasper while right leads to Wabasso Lake in about 5.5 km.

2. Keep straight on trail #9a. Climb to a junction, the start of the loop around the lakes. You can hike the circuit either way. I prefer clockwise for the best views.

3. Keep left. Cross a ridge and descend to the southeast end of First Lake. Bear right and arrive at a junction. The trail to the left leads to the far end of First Lake and continues through forest to Old Fort Point. Turn right.

4. The trail (#9a) now crosses open hillside above Second, Third and Fourth lakes to a junction between Fourth and Fifth lakes. If you turn right you can shorten the circuit by 1.8 km. The point of land between Third and Fourth lakes makes a good lunch spot.

5. Keep left and make a circuit of Fifth Lake on a narrower trail. Arrive back at a junction between Fourth and Fifth lakes just above the bridge over the creek.

6. Turn left, bearing left when in doubt, to reach the junction at the beginning of the circuit (2).

7. Keep left and follow trail #9a back to the parking lot.

Top: The boardwalk across Wabasso Creek (1).
Bottom: Beavers have been busy alongside the trail working at felling this 15″ diameter tree.

123

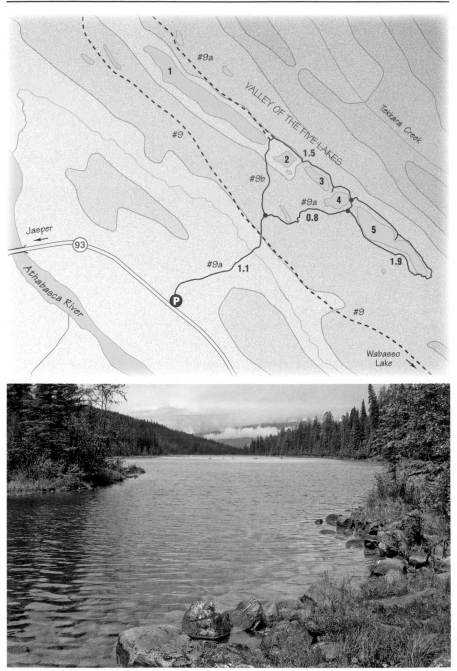

First Lake looking northwest.

Dry conditions in recent years have reduced Second and Third Lake to small ponds. This photograph was taken in mid-June (2007) when you would expect water levels to be high.

Fourth Lake taken in the early nineties when water levels in the area were much higher.

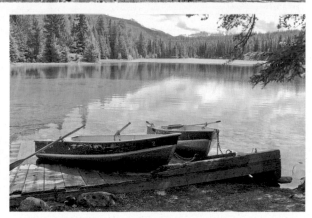

Looking down Fifth Lake. The boats in the foreground can be rented for fishing from Online Sport & Tackle or Currie's Guiding in Jasper.

32 Mina Lake–Riley Lake Circuit

Distance 9 km return
Height gain 230 m
High point 1290 m
Fairly easy
Year-round

Scenic lakes that can be easily reached from Jasper by those without their own transportation. Birdwatchers and photographers will enjoy Cottonwood Slough.

Start: From the information centre in Jasper, head north on Elm St. (immediately to the west) to Pyramid Lake Road. Turn right. The trailhead is at the back of a large parking lot opposite the Aquatic Centre.

Difficulty: Well-maintained trail, moderately steep at first. These trails are part of the Jasper numbered trails system. You will be following trails #8 and #2.

1. The trail is a few metres up the bank above the back of the parking lot. Head left behind townhouses and uphill through forest. At a junction stay right. Cross the Cabin Lake Service Road and continue on trail #8, ignoring any junctions. Pass a small slough and arrive at Mina Lake.

2. Continue along the shore of Mina Lake to a junction. Cabin Lake is 0.8 km to the left if you wish to extend your hike and visit it.

3. Turn right and follow trail #8, keeping left at a junction with trail #8c, which leads back through forest to Cabin Lake Service Road. Arrive at Riley Lake.

4. Continue around the end of Riley Lake turning right on trail #8 at the next junction. Descend through forest and follow the trail alongside Cottonwood Slough, the best bird watching and beaver habitat around Jasper, back to a small parking lot off Pyramid Lake Road.

5. Turn right onto trail #2. Cross Cabin Lake Service Road and go straight at the junction with #8c. After a short uphill, begin a long descent to the parking lot opposite the Aquatic Centre.

Mina Lake.

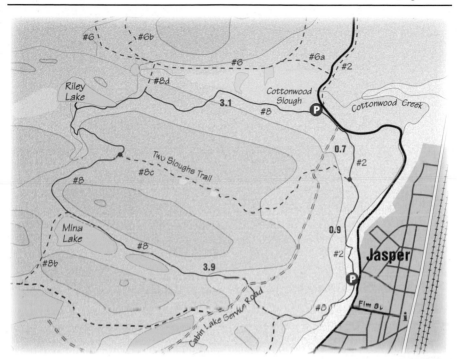

Options

While I have described one of the more popular circuits in the area, you can see from the map above that there are many options. All the trails are well signed.

• At the end of Minah Lake you can turn left and visit Cabin Lake. You should probably return the same way, as the wide swath of the Cabin Lake Service Road does not make for good hiking.

• You can extend your walk to take in Patricia Lake by following #8d to the Patricia Lake Circle Trail (#6) instead of turning right on #8. When you reach #6 you have the choice of turning right along the north side of Cottonwood Slough, or heading left to Patricia Lake. Return using #2 or head south on #6 to #6a.

• Trails farther north between Patricia and Pyramid lakes see heavy horse traffic.

The small slough on the way to Mina Lake.

Riley Lake.

Centre: Cottonwood Slough with Pyramid Mountain in the background.

Cabin Lake Service Road runs through the wide firebreak protecting the town of Jasper.

33 Opal Hills

Distance 8.2 km
Height gain 470 m
High point 2160 m
Fairly easy
No dogs
Mid-July to mid-September

The Opal Hills were named by Mary Schäffer in 1908 for the opal-like colours of the abundant wildflowers she found there. Shorter, but steeper, than the Bald Hills trail.

Start: From Jasper east entrance, drive east on Hwy. 16 for 1.8 km to the Maligne Lake Road. Turn right and cross the bridge over the Athabasca River. Shortly after, bear left at a junction and drive about 44 km to Maligne Lake. Turn left into the main parking lot and bus drop-off just before the lodge. Keep left and drive to the highest parking lot. The trailhead is straight ahead as you enter the lot.

Difficulty: A relentlessly steep trail to start, then a gentle walk down an alpine valley behind two small hills.

1. From the parking area the trail descends slightly to cross a boggy meadow. Pass a junction with Lakeshore Trail and arrive at a junction with the Mary Schäffer Loop. Fork left.

2. The trail enters the forest of dense lodgepole pines and climbs relentlessly to a junction—the start of the actual loop.

You have a choice here. The right-hand trail is very steep but gets you above treeline sooner. The left-hand trail is less steep and the valley walk affords better views.

3. I prefer to head left through forest and flowery subalpine glades to treeline where the trail heads to the right and enters a valley behind two low hills.

4. Hike gently downhill toward a creek coming in from the left. As you approach the creek you will notice that there appear to be three different trails ahead. You want to end up on the highest one.

5. Just after crossing the creek head slightly left and up to the highest trail.

6. The trail to the left leads back to the creek where there is a fork (the left-hand trail is a scramblers trail to Opal Peak, while the trail to the right soon peters out in flower meadows by some small cascades). Turn right and arrive at a signed four-way junction in 200 m.

7. The trail straight ahead is overgrown and not recommended. To get a view down to Maligne Lake and across to mounts Unwin and Charlton turn left and climb steeply up the ridge for about 400 m and follow a short trail to the right to a good viewpoint. See the option for the continuation of the trail up the ridge.

8. Back at the four-way junction continue straight ahead and follow the main trail very steeply down to the junction that ends the loop. Turn left and descend to the parking lot.

A wary mule deer a short way up the trail.

129

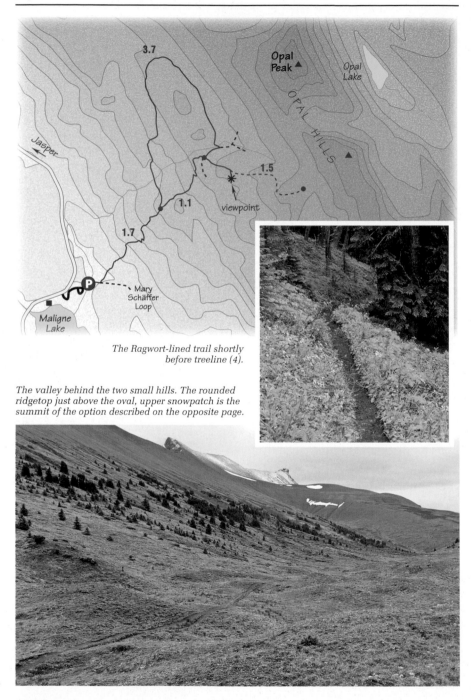

The Ragwort-lined trail shortly before treeline (4).

The valley behind the two small hills. The rounded ridgetop just above the oval, upper snowpatch is the summit of the option described on the opposite page.

Looking down on the two small hills from flower meadows by the creek (6).

Option Opal Ridge

Distance add 3 km return
Height gain add 300 m

This option extends your hike to a small grassy summit with good views.

1. From the four-way junction, follow the trail up the ridge with ever-improving views of Maligne Lake and across to the Bald Hills. The ridge ends on a small knoll.

2. Head right, picking your way over small scree and trending rightward to the ridge overlooking Maligne Lake. Follow this around to the left up easy scree to a small grassy summit—an outlier of the higher unnamed peak above.

3. Return the way you came.

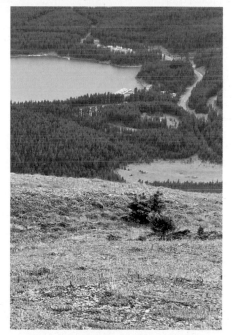

The north end of Maligne Lake from the ridge leading to the grassy summit (O2).

34 Bald Hills

Distance 12.5 km
Height gain 640 m
High point 2330 m
Moderately strenuous
No dogs
Mid-July to mid-September

Superb views of Maligne Lake. Open subalpine wildflower meadows allow you to wander to higher viewpoints.

Start: From Jasper east entrance, drive east on Hwy. 16 for 1.8 km to the Maligne Lake Road. Turn right and cross the bridge over the Athabasca River. Shortly after bear left at a junction and drive about 44 km to Maligne Lake. Follow the road to its end at a parking lot. The trailhead is the gated old fire road to you right as you turn into the parking lot.

Difficulty: The broad dirt road climbs easily and steadily all the way with an option at one point of a steeper short-cut.

1. The trail climbs steadily through an open forest of lodgepole pine. Ignore all side trails and keep your eyes open for a signed junction with a narrow trail to the left at 2.5 km.

2. You have two alternatives here. The trail to the left is steeper and shorter, the one to the right easier, though longer. I suggest you head right, leaving the steeper trail for the descent.

3. Continue on the fire road passing a junction with the Evelyn Creek Loop trail on your right. Arrive at the site of an old fire lookout (horse rail) with limited views of Maligne Lake. Look for the signed upper junction of the shortcut trail 90 m beyond the lookout site—your descent route.

4. After a breather, follow the trail southward to the foot of a small, rounded summit, then zigzag steeply to the top.

5. The small, rocky peak to the south with a cairn on top is a worthy objective. There is a good trail to the top.

6. Retrace your steps to the previously noted junction and follow the shortcut trail down to the fire road.

Maligne Lake from the rounded summit (4). The high mountain is Samson Peak with snow-covered Malign Mountain to its right.

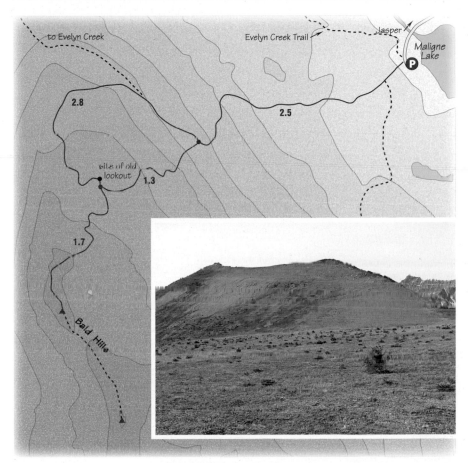

Above: The small, rocky peak (5) from the rounded summit (4). It's an easy walk to the top, and well worth it.

Mount Charlton (left) and Mount Unwin from the rocky peak (5). The peaks in the distance are the Mount Brazeau group beyond the south end of Maligne Lake.

133

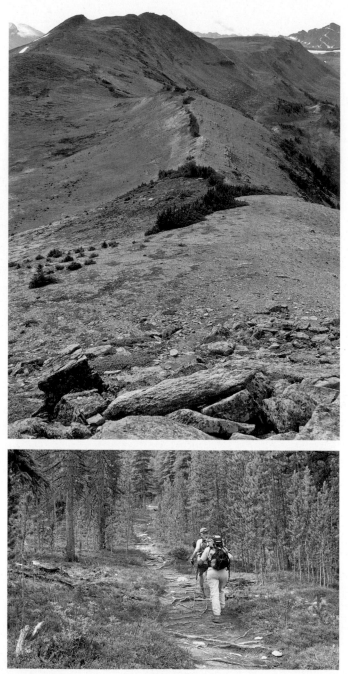

Looking south along the ridge from the summit of the small, rocky peak (5). It is possible to extend your hike along the ridge and explore the high alpine country beyond.

Nearing the bottom of the short-cut trail (6). The trail, originally a horse trail, is a little rooty in places but saves you 1.5 km.

35 *Little Shovel Pass*

Distance 21 km return
Height gain 550 m
High point 2240 m
Strenuous
No dogs
July to end of September

A shaded forest walk to a high pass set in open flower meadows and alpine tundra, with the option of a scenic ridgewalk.

Start: From Jasper east entrance, drive east on Hwy 16 for 1.8 km to the Maligne Lake Road. Turn right and cross the bridge over the Athabasca River. Shortly after bear left at a junction and drive about 44 km to Maligne Lake. Follow the road to its end at a parking lot. There are two trailheads on your right as you turn in to the parking lot. The one you want is to the right. The other gated dirt road leads up to The Bald Hills.

Difficulty: The trail is well graded and climbs gently for the first 5 km. It then switchbacks more steeply, breaking out of the trees a little way beyond Little Shovel campground. This is a long day out, so start early.

1. From the trailhead the trail follows a gentle grade all the way to the Evelyn Creek campground. On the way it passes a junction to Lorraine Lake, which is 140 m away to the left, and a little farther on, a junction to Mona Lake 200 m to the right. Neither lake is particularly interesting.

2. From Evelyn Creek campground the trail, still in the trees, begins to switchback more steeply, reaching Little Shovel campground at just under 8 km.

3. Continuing upward, the trail breaks out of the trees, affording outstanding views as you approach the pass.

4. Once at the pass consider ascending the small, unnamed peak to the northeast. See option.

5. Return the way you came.

Approaching Little Shovel Pass.

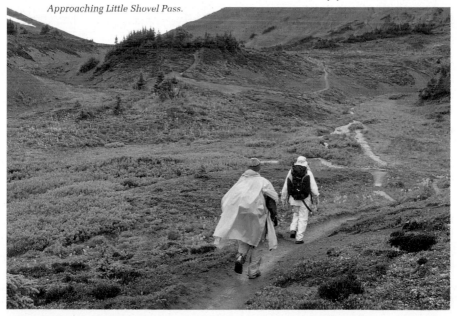

Option: A scenic ridgewalk

Distance add 1.1 km
Height gain add 240 m
High point 2480 m

The ridge to the northeast of Little Shovel Pass provides a scenic ridgewalk with views of the open tundra hereabouts that provides grazing for a small Caribou herd.

1. From the pass ascend grass and scree slopes to the northeast, working your way up onto a small rocky peak at the end of a short ridge.

2. At the far end of the ridge drop down to a rounded knoll, then head directly south following open ground down toward the main trail. On the opposite side of the valley are two prominent creeks. Lower down you should be descending an open ridge that points directly between the two creeks.

3. When you get to the trees contour to the right keeping to the open as much as possible until you arrive at the main trail.

The rocky peak at the end of the ridge (O1). The finger rock on the cairn points to Big Shovel Pass, on the route of the Skyline Trail.

Jasper

Evelyn Creek

Evelyn
Creek

4.0

Mona
Lake

Maligne River

5.0

Lorraine
Lake

Maligne Lake
Lodge

to Bald Hills
trail 2.2 km

P

Looking into the head of Snow Bowl from the rocky peak. The top of Mount Hardisty can be seen above the long ridge of the Maligne Range. Few people stop to explore these high alpine cirques.

The descent route from the southeast end of the ridge follows the open slopes down to the forested valley.

137

36 *Sulphur Skyline*

Distance 9.4 km return
Height gain 640 m
High point 2050 m
Moderate
Miette Hotsprings Road is open
from mid-May to early October

Start: From Jasper, follow Hwy. 16 east for about 40 km to the Miette Hotsprings Road at Pocahontas. If you are coming from the Edmonton direction, the junction is 7 km from Jasper Park east gate. Turn south and drive 17 km to the Miette Hotsprings. Park at the far end of the parking lot. The trailhead is to the right of the pool complex at the head of the drop-off loop.

Difficulty: A steady, steep, dry ascent on a well-graded trail with a steep final scramble up a stony path to the summit. There are lots of seats on the way.

Caution: Do not attempt to descend the northwest ridge to the hot springs. You will encounter steep, loose, dangerous terrain and miserable forest with cliffbands.

Stunning views of the serrated limestone ranges of eastern Jasper National Park. Your reward: a soak in the Miette Hot Springs pool.

1. Follow the wide, paved path steadily uphill. The paving ends and the trail narrows, climbing relentlessly to a junction. Left is Fiddle River and Mystery Lake. Keep straight on.

2. The trail continues steeply with many leg-aching switchbacks compensated for by views opening up across flower-filled meadows. Finally the trail levels off on a broad shoulder below the summit. Note the large, white boulder.

3. It's an easy walk across a small meadow to the final scramble to the summit where you are rewarded with a stunning view. To the southeast is the gravelly valley of the Fiddle River. South and west is the Miette Range and to the northwest the steeply tilted limestone of Ashlar Ridge.

4. Return the way you came.

The trail heads up onto the summit cone from the shoulder. The large boulder of white quartzite is a glacial erratic that was deposited here during the ice ages.

Expansive views open up to the southeast.

Bighorn sheep on the ridge leading to the summit.

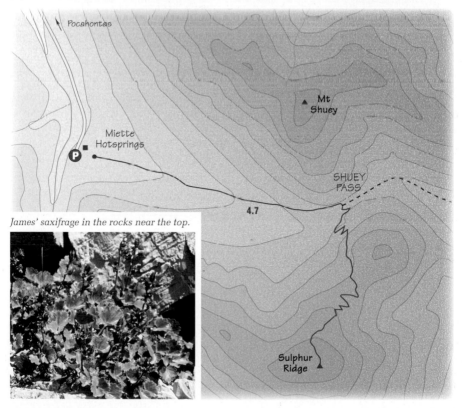

James' saxifrage in the rocks near the top.

Top: Looking down from the summit into the Fiddle River valley.

From the summit you can see a tempting ridge below with a trail along it. I don't recommend this as a way to descend. See the note on the previous page. If you do decide to hike the ridge you should return by the same route. It may be possible to traverse below the summit on a sheep trail to your ascent trail. I haven't done it.

37 Virl, Dorothy & Christine Lakes

Distance 10.1 km return
Height gain 275 m
High point 1340 m
Fairly easy
Mid-June to end of September

These low-elevation, forest-enclosed lakes are less crowded than trails closer to Jasper and offer early and late season hiking or respite from the sun on a very hot day.

Start: From the junction of the Icefields Parkway and Hwy. 16 in Jasper, head west on Hwy. 16 for 11.1 km to a small unsigned parking area on the right (north) just after Meadow Creek Bridge.

Difficulty: Easy walking on a well-established trail. Steep in places.

1. The trail starts on the railway service road. After 150 m climb the bank and cross the tracks at a X-ing sign and descend to the Miette River.

2. Cross the bridge and follow the trail (old wagon road) up the valley, then switchback and cross over a timbered ridge to the Minaga Creek drainage. Descend to the bridge over Minaga Creek.

The Miette River from the bridge.

3. About 400 m beyond the bridge over Minaga Creek you reach a junction. Keep right. The left-hand branch leads to Elysium Pass some 12 km away.

4. Hike gradually uphill for another kilometre to another junction. Follow the main trail straight ahead (#3e) to Dorothy Lake, the largest of the three lakes. Christine Lake, with its many little islands, is a short distance beyond Dorothy Lake. Follow a bushy trail along the shore to a good viewpoint near two islands.

5. Retrace your steps to the junction where a short side trail (#3f) leads left for 450 m to Virl Lake. This long slender lake has views to Indian Ridge and Muhigan Mountain.

6. Return the way you came.

Saskatoon in blossom. The berries provide food for foraging bears as well as chipmunks, squirrels and many woodland birds. Deer, elk and moose eat the leaves and twigs.

Dorothy Lake.

Christine Lake.

Virl Lake with The Whistlers and Indian Ridge in the background.

Phone Numbers and Contact Information

Banff National Park Information Centre
www.pc.gc.ca/pn-np/ab/banff/
224 Banff Avenue, in the Town of Banff
Phone: 403-762-1550

Lake Louise Visitor Centre
Village of Lake Louise, next to the Samson Mall
Phone: 403-522-3833
Trails Office: 403-522-1264

Kootenay National Park Visitor Centre
Located in Radium Hot Springs, B.C.
www.pc.gc.ca/pn-np/bc/kootenay/
Telephone 250.347.9505

Kootenay Park Lodge Visitor Centre
68 km (45 minutes) north of Radium Hot
Spring on Highway 93.
Phone: 403.762.9196

Yoho National Park Visitor Centre
Located at entrance to Town of Field
Phone: 250-343-6783
www.pc.gc.ca/pn-np/bc/yoho/

Jasper National Park Information Centre
Located about halfway along the main
street in Jasper
www.pc.gc.ca/pn-np/ab/jasper/
Phone: 780-852-6176
Trail Office: 780-852-6177

Icefield Centre information desk
Located at the Columbia Icefield
Phone: 780-852-6288

The Alpine Club of Canada
Phone: 403-678-3200
www.alpineclubofcanada.ca.

White Mountain Adventures
Phone: 403-762-7889
www.whitemountainadventures.com

Banff Transit
www.banff.ca/locals-residents/public-transit-buses.htm

Lake O'Hara Bus
To book a spot on the bus call Parks Canada
at 250-343-6433

Yoho-Burgess Shale Foundation
Phone: 1-800-343-3006.
www.burgess-shale.bc.ca/hikes.php

Valley of Five Lakes Boat Rental
Online Sport and Tackle, Jasper
Phone: 780-852-3630

Acknowledgments

Thank you to Gillian Ford for the photo on page 20 and an especial thanks to my wife, Gillean for the many photos not credited separately. You can tell which are hers: they are the best ones.

EMERGENCY
Dial 911

Disclaimer

There are inherent risks in hiking mountain areas that require hikers to constantly use their own judgment. Anyone using this book does so entirely at their own risk and both the author and the publisher disclaim any liability for any injuries or other damage that may be sustained by anyone hiking any of the trails described in this book.

Be aware that bear sightings and fire hazard can close trails at a moment's notice. Flash floods can wash out bridges. Fallen trees resulting from strong chinook winds can block trails and make the going difficult.

In this book there are no dos or don'ts. It is assumed that users are caring, intelligent people who will respect the country they are travelling through and its wildlife.